THE HOLLYWOOD MBA

ALSO BY TOM REILLY

The Big Picture

THE
HOLLYWOOD
MBA

A CRASH COURSE IN
MANAGEMENT FROM A LIFE
IN THE FILM BUSINESS

TOM REILLY

St. Martin's Press 🙢 New York

THE HOLLYWOOD MBA. Copyright © 2016 by Tom Reilly. All rights reserved. Printed in the United States of America. For information, address St. Martin's Press, 175 Fifth Avenue, New York, N.Y. 10010.

www.stmartins.com

Designed by Patrice Sheridan

The Library of Congress Cataloging-in-Publication Data is available upon request.

ISBN 978-1-250-09918-1 (hardcover)
ISBN 978-1-250-09919-8 (e-book)

Our books may be purchased in bulk for promotional, educational, or business use. Please contact your local bookseller or the Macmillan Corporate and Premium Sales Department at 1-800-221-7945, extension 5442, or by e-mail at MacmillanSpecialMarkets@macmillan.com.

First Edition: January 2017

10 9 8 7 6 5 4 3 2 1

For Kathy

CONTENTS

———★———

ACKNOWLEDGMENTS

★

I OWE A huge debt of gratitude to the thousands of filmmaking professionals I spent decades working alongside who taught me so much about the art and craft of filmmaking and the business value of great leadership. I am especially grateful to the many mentors who took the time to help guide me early in my career—Bobby Greenhut, Woody Allen, Gordon Willis, Mike Rauch, Charles Okun, Fred Caruso, Mike Peyser, Alan Hopkins, and Laurie Eichengreen, among others.

I also want to give a heartfelt thanks to the many friends and colleagues I met along the way—Jim Mazzola, Bobby Ward, the Quinlans and Sabats, Brian Hamill, Joe Hartwick, the Salad sisters, Red Burke, Ron Petagna, Mike Green, Santo Loquasto, and dozens more not mentioned here—you know who you are. It was a privilege and honor, and you made it fun.

Many thanks to my literary agent, Leah Spiro, at Riverside Creative Management for her unflagging determination and guidance; she has been a superb advocate on my behalf throughout the process of writing this book. And of course a special thank-you to my editor, Tim Bartlett, for his sage insight and wisdom—which are so greatly appreciated—and to Annabella, Laura, and the rest of the team at St. Martin's Press for their input and professionalism.

Finally, I'd like to thank my wife, Kathy; my children, James, Kate, and Mackenzie, for their endless love, support, and inspiration; my parents, Ann and Jim, who taught me the value of hard work and education; and my brother, Phil, for always being there. It has been a journey, and I was lucky to take it with all of you.

PREFACE

★

IMAGINE THAT YOUR phone rings and a start-up company offers to hire you to manage and lead a project that begins immediately. You will have $60 million in operating capital and are being contracted to manufacture *a single product*. The entire process will take approximately six months. You will be given a blueprint for making this product, but it won't contain precise measurements or detailed instructions, yet your first task will be to use this *nonspecific* blueprint to draft a *very specific* business plan, including a manufacturing schedule and a detailed budget.

Note that this product can't be manufactured in a single location, and there is no facility set up to produce it anywhere in the world. In fact, it will have to be assembled piecemeal, possibly in a hundred or more different locations—not all of which will necessarily be on the same continent. Some component parts of this product will have to be manufactured outside in the elements, and you will need to keep in mind that some of these manufacturing sites may be hard to navigate—even dangerous. They may involve being underwater, out to sea, inside airplanes, or on top of buildings. And each manufacturing site will require all sorts of special tools and materials—from concrete and steel to cranes, helicopters, and explosives. Other components of this single, $60 million product will have to be manufactured indoors in one or more makeshift "factories" that the employees of this start-up company will have to build themselves—on the fly.

Manufacturing this single product will require a hundred or more experienced, freelance, full-time, highly skilled professionals to travel to all these locations as a group, as well as several thousand part-time employees, most of whom will be represented by one of ten or more labor unions with requisite mandates to work around, and diverse and sometimes competing and contradictory rules—all of which will be outlined in lengthy contracts. On top of the union rules, there will be local, state, federal, and international laws as well as OSHA regulations to consider to boot, and since all those contractual mandates, laws, and regulations carry weighty penalties if they are violated, even a small miscue or error in judgment can be costly. Plus, some key employees may not speak English, and it's highly unlikely that more than a handful of the team you will assemble to work on this project will have worked together before—so hiccups and glitches and less-than-seamless integration are to be expected.

There will be a precise schedule for manufacturing each of the product's component parts, and if you fall behind, even by a few days, you will lose hundreds of thousands of dollars from your budget. Your production costs will run in the vicinity of $20,000 an hour, or just over $300 a minute, so "hurry up" will be the rule of the day, as any amount of lag time, downtime, or otherwise wasted time will eat away at your budget in a very linear and painfully quantifiable fashion. And unlike many other industries, *once the clock starts ticking, neither the dollars nor the days will be recoupable.*

As with just about any other manufactured good, the ultimate success of this enterprise will depend on the quality and commercial viability of the finished product, which means that there will be a constant battle between the technical and creative quality of your output, the speed of production, and dollars spent—a set of dynamics that will lead you, as a manager, to spend an unhealthy amount of time thinking about efficiency as it relates to even *minuscule* segments of time.

Additionally, since you will be manufacturing *a single, $60 million product*, there will be a bevy of overseers, many of whom will be in offices thousands of miles away and have little idea how to manufacture this product themselves. Unfortunately, that fact will not deter them from frequently—and forcefully—offering their opinions as to how *you* should proceed; after all, they've put a lot of eggs (dollars, reputations, and careers) in one basket (you and your team). Be prepared that these overseers will get—and perhaps rightfully so—demanding and volatile as problems arise, so plan on doing—and listening to—a *lot* of explaining, justifying, negotiating, and manipulating. It's a complicated, stressful relationship; you may be the one tasked with leading the team in manufacturing this product, but you are spending *their* money to do so.

As with most start-ups, the hours will be brutal. As a minimum, twelve to fourteen hours a day should be expected—and not all of them will be during daylight hours or close to home, so virtually everyone involved will be sleep deprived, physically drained, and mentally fatigued for most of the process, as well. If this sounds a bit extreme—even crazy—it's because it is. And that's precisely what makes this $100 billion global industry such a great source for management and leadership case studies.

> *The single $60 million product I am describing is a feature film—a major motion picture—and the blueprint that you were given was the script.*

INTRODUCTION

———————★———————

MacArthur Causeway Bridge, Miami Beach
10:00 P.M.

ONE NIGHT IN 1994, I found myself standing all alone in the middle of the shut-down MacArthur Causeway, a six-lane highway that connects the city of Miami Beach to the mainland via a double-leaf drawbridge. As I was looking out over Biscayne Bay and the Miami skyline, reflecting on what we were about to do and the role I would play in it, I was thinking that there isn't another product that is manufactured with the same level of fragmented, incremental, and synchronized *live effort* than a major motion picture. It was day six of a tough car chase sequence that was about to culminate with an open bridge jump for the Warner Bros. picture *Just Cause* starring Sean Connery; a film budgeted at $60 million with fifty-three shooting days spread out between a number of locations in Florida and a few in Cambridge, Massachusetts. We had been shooting the previous five nights using more than twenty stunt drivers and stunt doubles as the driver of the lead vehicle tore through the streets of Miami Beach in a tricked-out car weaving in and out of oncoming traffic at high speed, driving on the wrong side of the road along a meticulously planned route that went from the Eden Roc hotel, headed up Collins Avenue, and then onto the MacArthur Causeway.

But that was a cakewalk compared to what we were about to do now.

It was jump night—just three hours until go time—and I was responsible for leading and managing the coordinated efforts of our regular 120-person first-unit* film crew, the stunt coordinator, the stunt driver who would actually fly the car over the open drawbridge, thirteen camera crews (to get all our coverage in one take), a chopper pilot (for aerial photography), a bridge operator (to control the double-leaf bascule bridge), dozens of Dade County Police (to lock up the highway and roads) and rescue divers standing by in a boat below the bridge (in case things went south).

The stunt driver was going to get behind the wheel of his car, positioned roughly three hundred yards out from the open drawbridge, and on my cue, he would floor it, then roar up the road, accelerate to 70 mph, climb the near side of the ramp that was elevated at a forty-five-degree incline, and soar over the open span nine stories above the water of Biscayne Bay. After a heart-stopping, airborne five seconds, he would land squarely on the roadway on the far side of the open bridge in a spray of sparks, bounce, recover control of the car, barrel down the inclined section of road, and continue his high-speed getaway.

---

* *First unit* refers to the normal shooting crew that films all principal photography on a movie. *Second units* are sometimes used to get additional coverage that doesn't include the principal cast, insert photography, and sometimes stunt work outside of the regular shooting schedule.

Standing on that roadway just a few hours before the jump, I was acutely aware of the fact that for the night to go well, I had to have two distinct sets of finely honed skills.

First, I had to have advanced and sophisticated knowledge of feature filmmaking.

And second, I had to have superlative leadership and management skills.

What had surprised me early in my career was that as complicated and technical as the filmmaking aspects of my job were, it was the management and leadership skills that would prove to be far more elusive and much harder to master. And I was quick to realize that it was those management and leadership skills that would make or break my career; that no matter how much I knew about the technical craft of filmmaking,[†] my ability to manage and lead would overshadow everything else. This is a dynamic not unique to me. In fact, there are two specific reasons that this applies to *virtually everyone regardless of what field they happen to work in.*

The first is that for many of us, the technical skill set necessary for us to excel at our jobs is *inherently easier to learn* than is the less concrete nature of management and leadership.

The second is that we are specifically trained in how to do the *technical* side of our jobs, but we often are *not trained at all* in how to manage and lead.

[†] Google confirmed this observation in an internal management study called Project Oxygen, where they set out to determine which attributes were the most critical for good managers to have, and they found that relevant technical know-how was the least important factor of a successful team leader.

The paradox is that people are often promoted to management positions because *they are good at something that has little to do with management itself*. Then consider that virtually every one of us functions in the role of a manager at some point in our lives—in fact, we often do so across a variety of situations—and yet very few of us are actually taught the skills necessary to manage *at all*, let alone how to manage *well*.

And here's the kicker. Management skills make or break not only individual careers but companies, too.

When Gallup conducted a study of employee engagement, they examined roughly fifty thousand businesses in thirty-four countries that collectively had close to 1.5 million employees, and what they discovered was that companies with above-average employee engagement had *twice* the likelihood of success as those with below-average employee engagement. Companies at the ninety-ninth percentile of employee engagement had *quadruple* the success rate. And for good reason. High employee engagement increases profit, productivity, and quality of output as it decreases absenteeism, safety incidents, and employee turnover. Gallup estimates that 70 percent of the US workforce functions at a low level of engagement, and that costs businesses in the vicinity of $500 billion a year in lost revenue.

And what exactly improves employee engagement?

Effective supervisors and good management‡—*the very thing that so many of us struggle to get right.*

Two simple facts: to a large degree, your individual career will

---

‡ Gallup reports that managers account for 70 percent of variance in employee engagement.

likely succeed or fail based on your management and leadership skills, and the success of the company that employs you is equally dependent on how well *it* is managed.

So how do most of us learn management and leadership skills?

Unfortunately, for a lot of us, it's through painful trial and error—even for those with MBAs.

And we read. In my case, I read *everything I could get my hands on.*

Early in my career, I pushed my film books off to the side and began to read management and leadership books written by the greats—books by business legends, sports coaches, and military leaders. But it quickly became apparent that while these books offered general advice and were often inspirational—I mean, who doesn't love the maxims of George S. Patton, who gave us "A pint of sweat saves a gallon of blood" or "Success is how high you bounce when you hit bottom"?—they weren't providing me with the *actionable, easy-to-employ management and leadership strategies that would give me the results I wanted with the immediacy that I required.* And that's when it hit me.

What most of these existing books offered wasn't *specific* enough for what *I* needed.

And there's a reason for that, too.

Most businesses aren't conducted in the extreme conditions or the short time frames that feature filmmaking is.

So to do my job effectively, I found that I had no choice but to develop my own leadership and management tenets.

Here's why this matters to you: *the tenets I developed actually work, and not just when managing a film set.*

In fact, the motion picture industry is of particular interest as a source of insight into management and leadership directives for *three very specific reasons.*

The first is that film projects have a staggering number of diverse elements and component parts that often mandate working in *extreme conditions*—conditions that vary *constantly*—not just from project to project but day to day and even minute to minute. That means that we require strategies that are *extremely* effective.

The second reason is that when we use those strategies, we can actually tell—in real time—if they're working. And that fact provides tremendous incentive for us to make sure that they *do work.*

And the third reason is shared by research biologists who study the fruit fly—with a life span of only fourteen days, a fruit fly cycles through generations quickly. That means the fruit fly provides researchers with *rapid feedback loops. Scientists can test something, get results, modify their approach, and then test again.*

A film project essentially does the same thing—it goes from start-up to shutdown *really fast*—in just six months to a year— which means that just as the fruit fly offers biologists *a vehicle for cycling through generations—and modifications—quickly*, filmmaking offers a manager like me, who's looking to beta test new ideas and ways of doing things in business, *rapid feedback loops, too.*

What this means is that I was able to capitalize on the extreme nature and short feedback cycles of filmmaking to employ the agile development practices favored in the tech world—not to fine-tune a product but to develop a set of unique and highly honed management and leadership strategies that actually work.

And these leadership and management strategies happen to

work, not only in the extreme conditions that *I* face but also in more mundane situations that others face, as well.

Business schools have long established that the best way to teach, and the best way to learn, is with a curriculum based on documented case studies. And *the best case studies come from industries and brands that have faced a unique and particular set of challenges.* In fact, the best case studies offer narratives that fall a few standard deviations from the norm and promise aha moments. They're what Malcolm Gladwell would call outliers; they are extreme, dynamic, suspenseful, compelling, and memorable, presenting high stakes and big, quantifiable—and generalizable—outcomes. And that's precisely what I am offering here. Decisive, actionable, broadly applicable management and leadership tenets derived from case studies in an industry that has extreme outlier status.

So who am I, and what exactly do I do?

Once a film is green-lit, I am brought in as part of the production team that's tasked with planning, scheduling, and overseeing the project while making sure that it is of the highest creative quality and also delivered on time with no cost overruns, unnecessary artistic compromises, or untenable safety issues. I learned to lead and manage on the streets of New York—and at locations around the world, shooting films with budgets that ran $200,000 per shooting day. Over the years, I've managed more than fifty A-list projects and worked for all the major studios and with many of the top actors, directors, producers, and cinematographers in the world, including over seventy Academy Award winners. If they were prorated in today's dollars, those fifty projects would have racked up collective production budgets in excess of $2 billion and generated gross revenue well in excess of that.

In my job, I am essentially tasked with all the things that a corporate manager would normally deal with over the decades-long life cycle of a company, just minus the long-term vision statements and planning—everything from launch to personnel management, team building, day-to-day planning, scheduling, safety, concept execution, and innovation to the scaling of money, people, and time. And because the life cycle of a film project is measured in months, not decades, I was doing this within a *dramatically accelerated time frame—which means that because filmmaking is an outlier with a short business cycle and rapid feedback loops, I was able to try out a management strategy, see if it worked, and if it didn't, make adjustments and try over (and over) again until I found what did work.*

Running large-scale film crews on soundstages and on location with one eye on cost control and the other on quality of output, wielding a stopwatch, and a sense of fair play—coupled with a love of the art—I developed strategies to keep a large workforce on schedule and on budget project after project, year after year. In fact, inclusive of cast and crews, during my career as a first assistant director, production manager, and associate producer, I've been responsible for overseeing somewhere in the vicinity of one hundred thousand employees. And what I learned was that to do my job well, I needed to become, above all else, an Oscar-worthy *manager.*

When I talk to managers or read about the corporate challenges and pain points team leaders and CEOs working in more traditional industries—and circumstances—face, I understand that very few people have the management experience—or perspective—that I do. *Think about it; if you had managed fifty rapid-cycle start-up projects over thirty years, you'd have recognized patterns, seen what worked and what didn't—and done it fast—too.*

So, faced with the challenge of managing and leading large work crews in a business defined by extremes, I set out to find the small and relatively easy-to-implement management strategies that I could employ to effectively change outcomes for the better, and in the process, I spent a lot of time thinking about *inefficiency* and how to eliminate—or at least diminish—it. Take, for example, the assembly-line worker at Harley Davidson who deduced that the 1.2 extra seconds it took to snap in a poorly designed motorcycle part resulted in lowered annual production of 2,200 units and therefore millions of dollars in lost revenue for the company over the course of each and every year—I was looking to isolate management and leadership changes on *that* scale.

I was looking for small changes that lead to big results.

Here's the good news—*I found them.*

And the best part is that the strategies I developed are universally applicable to virtually every other business and management situation where the goal is better return on investment (ROI), facilitated work flow, tighter cost and quality control, increased output, reduced friction, a high degree of safety, greater employee job satisfaction, low stress, and the highest possible quality product or service.

But if you're not convinced that filmmaking offers a treasure trove of management and leadership challenges and directives, just consider the following scenario:

You being me for a single day. But this time you're not about to jump a car over an open drawbridge at 70 mph. On this day, for that same project, you're filming in an alligator-infested swamp.

YOU'VE READ THE best-of-the-best management and leadership books out there. In fact, you've scribbled directives from some of those books on the palms of your hands—hell, they're inked halfway up your arms. *Commitment. Passion. Trust. Make decisions slowly by consensus. Level out the workload* . . . But you're not on a factory floor or in some cushy corner office with a water cooler, Nespresso machine, wellness room, and air-conditioning. Today's "office," where you are managing a hundred-person crew who are toiling under enormously difficult conditions, is in the Florida Everglades, and you're standing knee-deep in a swamp in 110-degree heat, getting ready to photograph the first scene of the day on a major motion picture for Warner Bros.

Your $10 million leading man, Sean Connery, has just exited the makeup-and-hair camper looking like the next cover model for an Abercrombie & Kent brochure for fly fishing in exotic locales. He's about to step into water that would, under normal circumstances, be infested with the fiercest of predators—the American alligator—a reptile that can reach fifteen feet in length and weigh a thousand pounds. The aptly named "lord of the swamp," (the gator, not Sean) you've been told, has a bone-crushing bite force of 2,980 pounds per square inch (psi)—higher by far than that of a hippo (1,821 psi), gorilla (1,300 psi), tiger (1,050 psi), or even a car-crushing machine (2,400 psi). The alligator wranglers carrying side arms and high-powered rifles that you insisted on having on set "just in case" bolster your confidence; after all, they've assured you that the area of the swamp where you are filming has been cleared of gators and (most) snakes, but you're still on edge.

Along with the alligators, there are black widow spiders, fire ants, water moccasins, scorpions, swarms of mosquitos—*nothing friendly here*. In fact, every living thing in the Everglades has been designed by nature with a very basic goal: *Kill. Eat. Reproduce. Repeat.*

When you scouted this location a couple of months back, you counted over two hundred alligators within a hundred meters of where you were standing. As you stepped near the shore that day, they silently, and en masse, eased into the water and started gliding toward you. You were thinking, *This looks like . . . well . . . a movie.* But you were quite sure the gators were thinking something far more prosaic—*that their lunch had arrived—and it's you.*

Now, eight weeks later, you're back in the same spot with that hundred-person crew and ten tons of equipment brought in by a half dozen trucks and the same number of motor homes and vans. But unlike Sean Connery, who's been in an air-conditioned motor home and is cool, ironed, and coiffed in the muggy, triple-digit heat, you, along with the crew, have already sweated through your clothes and have that unpleasant, sticky feeling of sunscreen mixed with insect repellent mixed with exhaustion and stress. You're working with one eye focused on the swamp, since alligators can run faster than a man, and you're responsible for everyone on set. Plus, you were told it's mating season—alligator mating season, that is—which means that you can expect an even higher level of aggressive behavior than "normal."

As you look around the swamp, the grip and camera departments have just finished rigging a Technocrane that will arm out over the water, the director is pacing back and forth, the director of photography (DP, or cinematographer), whose English is limited under normal circumstances, is having an even tougher time than usual understanding the lingo of the Everglades and keeps asking, to no avail, for the term *water moccasin* to be translated into Hungarian. You're standing at the camera, the epicenter of activity where most of the decisions are made, surrounded by a small army of people working feverishly so that the two actors who will be in front of the camera (Sean Connery and Laurence Fishburne) will be able to give their best performance in these adverse circumstances. As you plow through your day running the set, knowing that every single decision and buck stops with you, you are taking into consideration dozens of constantly changing variables that affect your work in uniquely debilitating ways. And when you look down at your arm where you inked those tips from the management books that you've read over the years, you realize that there's no way any of *that* advice—*Set goals for your employees! Look for opportunities to give praise! Don't micromanage!*—is going to get you through a day like this.

As if the heat and the swamp teeming with voracious mosquitoes, alligators, and venomous snakes aren't bad enough, the clock is running at $20,000 per hour like some unrelenting fiscal timekeeper of doom. And you know that the money isn't the only thing ticking like a time bomb. The earth is rotating, too. (This is significant because photography is light dependent, and the sun is critical for your work.) It may only be 9:07 A.M. in Florida, but the clock started running on the light at 7:00 A.M. when you left the hotel this morning and headed to this location, and it will continue to do so until it sets at 7:54 P.M. The union clock is running its meter, too—double time kicks in for the crew after eleven hours—so you will have to make sure that you arrive back in Miami, where the cast and crew are housed, by 7:00 P.M. Allowing an hour to load the trucks after you wrap shooting and an hour for travel means that you can only film until 5:00 P.M. You also need to break the crew for lunch for an hour by 1:00 P.M. (more union rules), so even though it's early in the morning, you're thinking far ahead, watching the time and making sure you hit your targets—which means cultivating an environment conducive to artistic work while shooting two and a half pages of the script, abiding by union rules, and staying on budget. Factored into the equation, among numerous other considerations, is that whenever you move to a new location (often daily), you are relocating one hundred men and women, dozens of cars, a caterer, honey wagons (bathrooms), a half dozen trucks, five motor homes, six vans, and a couple of flatbed trucks and cranes, and, in this case, an ambulance and EMTs equipped with snakebite kits.

Then there are the union rules about hours worked and the number of men on the job, along with the actors' schedules to consider, as well. Sean, for example, has to fly—via private jet—to the Bahamas every Friday *by contract* (if he doesn't, he could face costly US income tax ramifications), and it seems there's never an airport close enough to where you're shooting. Plus, he has a hard out date of August 1 because he is to start work on a new picture in London that week. If you run over on his time, the penalty the company would have to pay will be *$200,000 per day*. As you're thinking about all of this, you have a huge crew to manage (half of whom appear to be standing thigh high in the reeds and looking fatigued and miserable already) as you try to get the day's work done without anyone getting eaten or dismembered, to say nothing of accomplishing the end goal—capturing a few minutes of film with brilliant performances by the actors, coupled with a flawless technical job by the crew.

On a positive note, by the time 1:00 P.M. rolls around and you break the crew for lunch, you're feeling pretty good—you've accomplished a half day's work as scheduled. You shot the sequence where Paul Armstrong (played by Sean Connery) discovers the murder weapon—a knife that's been stashed inside a culvert by a serial killer—and it went well, all things considered. Plus, the afternoon weather forecast seems hopeful (it rains almost daily during the summer in Florida, so time delays must be factored into your schedule). But 1:00 P.M. in Florida makes it 10:00 A.M. on the "left coast," and the studio executives in LA will want to check in with you to see how the day's work is going. Those executives at Warner's can't understand what it's like filming in the gator-infested sauna, so you won't bother them with the logistics the crew faced getting the equipment to where you were actually filming or the challenges they encountered when building the crane.[§] You won't bring up the extra time it took the electricians to run the cable through the reeds, or how dealing with the extreme heat and humidity meant a lot more time-consuming touch-ups for makeup and hair for Sean and Laurence after each and every take as well as wardrobe changes as needed as they sweated through

---

[§] The crane weighs about three thousand pounds, takes three men to assemble, and has a thirty-foot arm with a remote head to mount a camera on.

their shirts. You won't even tell them about the crew member who had to be medevaced out after he was bitten by a snake. Or about the seven-foot gator that the wranglers had to extract after it lunged ferociously out of a culvert, snapping and growling like a *T. rex* from a scene in *Jurassic Park*—the very culvert that Sean would be sticking his hand in to retrieve the knife. You don't bother reporting any of those details or the management challenges they posed because the guys at the studio merely want to know if you shot scene sixty-nine yet and if the afternoon's work looks promising. Since you did, and it does, you report that so far you're on schedule—after all, that's all they want to know. Then you get word from someone back at the office that one of the "suits" happened to mention that Steven Spielberg, husband of your leading lady, Kate Capshaw, may fly in the following week and drop by the set. And you're thinking, *That'll* really *relax the director.*

You've been at this location only a few hours and already know damn well there is nothing in all those management books that will help you navigate this swamp, the gators massing by the bridge, the IRS, OSHA, the setting sun, the unions, or the executives in LA, except perhaps one of your favorite "rally the troops" edicts from General George S. Patton, like "Pressure makes diamonds!" or perhaps "Accept the challenges so that you can feel the exhilaration of victory!" But even though these might shore you up, they provide little specific, *actionable* management and leadership direction—so you fall back on a few of your own.

IF YOU THINK the car chase and bridge jump or the alligator-swamp–Sean Connery situation are one-offs—they aren't. In fact, there're fairly typical. When Robert De Niro was about to dive into the Atlantic Ocean on the film *Great Expectations*, I made it a point to talk to him about all the hammerhead sharks that inhabited those Florida waters. We had a stunt double standing by, but Bob just gave me one of his looks. (After seeing *Raging Bull* or *Cape Fear*, you might pity the shark that bothers Bob.) We decided it was safe, and he did the shots himself—with our usual package of motorboats and standby divers—but you can see that the challenges we continue to face in the motion picture industry are anything but conventional.

I've had to figure out how to get cows into a Manhattan storefront (they don't like to climb stairs or ride in elevators), film an elephant on a beach on the Jersey shore, and dangle a ten-year-old kid out of a window on the fifth floor of an apartment building among thousands of other unconventional business tasks. Then, of course, there are the nude love scenes, helicopter shots, explosions, full-body fire burns, and stunt fights. And all these things are happening as I schedule the days of hundreds of people while staying mindful of the fact that we are spending $60 million in a matter of months. I'm talking maybe two hundred scenes to film on eighty locations with seventy actors and three thousand extras. We may be filming on a spaceship (built), or Normandy Beach (real), or in a state prison (real *and* unnerving); it matters not. The bottom line is that I am expected to play my part extremely well in an ever-changing, fluid environment. I must be an expert on *everything*, *exude* confidence, *instill* confidence, and above all make fast, hard decisions for the crew to follow. And if I don't know an answer, I have to make that clear . . . and then get one. In filmmaking, there is a staccato intensity and a mandate for certitude as these decisions are made. So I learned a thing or two about hiring, team building, leading, achievement, flexibility, employee relations, stalwart perseverance, hot and cold cognition,** goal-directed decision-making, and day-to-day management and crisis intervention, along with salesmanship, confidence, coercion, deference, "moving the chains," and humility over the years. And while most business leaders will never have to deal with the *specific* issues we deal with in film production, the *specific* methods employed to manage them apply across industries and to more quotidian circumstances.

Which begs the question:

How *exactly* do you build the kind of trust a manager needs leading up to moments like those that I have just described when so much is at stake?

Because that trust is the foundation for any manager or team leader in any business.

How do you architect a team and work environment where every member of your workforce has confidence that *every single detail of every element* of the project will be so well planned that the work will be accomplished as seamlessly—and executed as safely and as efficiently—as humanly possible? And how do you do it in a manner that affords all members of the team the individual freedoms and comforts *they* need to perform *their* jobs to their maximum technical and creative ability?

The Hollywood MBA will tell you. And it will also provide answers to questions like these:

** *Hot cognition* is emotional decision-making, and *cold cognition* is rational, calm decision-making.

How do you structure a broad management system that will *automate positive outcomes*?

How does one balance the *individual* needs of so many against the *collective* needs of the group and the project as a whole?

What is the key to improving functionality in industries with siloed departments?

Why is it important to recognize the significance of both *assigned* and *emergent* leaders in your workforce?

How *do you* build trust and confidence when you're thrown together with a new workforce time and again?

How do you consistently get peak performances out of your employees?

And because productivity is such a critical issue for *all* managers, how do you craft an environment that produces a highly engaged and self-motivated workforce by replicating what I call the "Oscar Effect"?

What is the complicated truth behind employee accommodations and benefits?

Why should you reframe how you think about diversity, and why is it so important that you do?

How *exactly* do you build equity in your workforce that you can cash in when times get tough?

How do you make decision-making easier and systematically cut short the life cycle of problems using what I call the "hard corner" approach?

How do you create a crisis-management model, and why is it so important?

What are the differences between *leading* and *managing*, and how do you effectively do *both*?

After all, every manager will face some, if not all, of these key questions, whether he or she is managing a feature film, a small business, a big business, a Fortune 500 company, a community group—or even a family.

INVERT CONTROL

———————————— ★ ————————————

Don't Call Us, We'll Call You

CASE STUDY:
The film *The Prince of Tides*. Warner Bros. Directed by Barbra Streisand; starring Barbra Streisand, Nick Nolte, and Blythe Danner.

ONE OF THE overriding challenges facing anyone running a company or heading up a division or a team—regardless of its size or the specific industry that it's in—is how to improve productivity and efficiency, even incrementally. This is a paramount focus in almost all businesses, but it is of particular concern in industries like film production where minutes matter and dollars add up very quickly and the cost can be high if we miss our marks even by a little. It's also particularly top-of-mind for us because, unlike many other businesses, in filmmaking, we *know at the end of any given day whether we are on schedule and on budget, and if we're not, we know how much we are behind or over.* That means that finding ways to improve our productivity and efficiency isn't just a top priority; *the imperative to do so is staring us right in the face.*

A key mistake that managers can make when working in businesses with less visible measures of productivity and efficiency is thinking, *If I can't see it, I can't fix it.* Or, *If I can't see it, it's not happening.* And a key insight that they often fail to realize is that these metrics *can* be improved—often significantly—with small changes in overall management strategies and their day-to-day implementation. To consider a simple example of just how big the impact of *a small change in management approach* or even a small change in *the specific language of a single directive* can be, take the cliché line Hollywood casting directors say to actors after an audition or casting call:

"Don't call us, we'll call you."

Those six words do something very powerful, something that any manager can relate to—*they save time and improve efficiency.*

"Don't call us, we'll call you" instantly takes the power and control *away from the actors and gives it to the casting directors.*

In other words, they *invert control.*

Because there will be far fewer incoming (and completely unproductive) phone calls from all the actors who didn't get the part, that statement immediately cuts down on work. And it does so with a single statement.

This concept is so powerful that when computer coders wrote a line of code that essentially did the same thing—inverted control and stopped inefficient contacts within a computer program— the coders jokingly called it *the Hollywood principle.*

Here's what those computer coders understood:

If they could write lines of computer code that would do what

"Don't call us, we'll call you" does—instantly invert control and automate better outcomes—they would have more efficient computer programs.

And here's the best part:

When you find ways to invert control with a single statement like this, you get *precisely what you want with very little effort*—and this is true whether you are a casting director, a computer coder, *or* a manager.

Or, to phrase it differently, employing the concept behind inversion of control and the Hollywood principle is a simple way for anyone to improve efficiency and productivity.

Recognizing both the simplicity and the impact of that concept, I asked myself this: *What if I took the construct of inversion of control that is embedded in the Hollywood principle and applied it to building a broad system of management that delivered similarly, highly efficient outcomes for all sorts of things?*

So as I learned and grew as a manager, as often as I could, I looked to embed broad procedures and coded "commands" that inverted control as they maximized efficiency, productivity, creativity, and innovation as a means to improve outcomes and bolster success—not to mention make my job as a manager easier.

And the results far exceeded what I had hoped for.

In other words, *it really worked*.

LET'S BEGIN WITH the *simplest* of simple examples of the Hollywood principle—or inversion of control—at work on a film set. Say we're shooting on the streets of New York City at rush hour in as-tough-as-they-get conditions, and over the walkie-talkie I hear a member of my production team say, "Someone go get my laptop bag." As a manager, I know that command will send a minimum of five people (production assistants, or PAs) running back to a motorhome blocks away *to retrieve a bag*. Since everyone on the team is trying very hard to get recognized for performance, they will all run to get that bag. But being "better" at retrieving a bag in this case is a function of *proximity* rather than *skill*—whoever is closer to the bag's location will be the one who retrieves it. So that instruction is, of course, extremely *inefficient*. I will have at least five team members who have left their positions unmanned, which could be problematic—and since only one person can actually get to the bag first, four of those team members won't accomplish *anything*. So, "Someone go get my laptop bag" is a line of code—or instruction—that isn't just *inefficient*, it creates *worthless competition, as it also sets us up for potential cascading problems*.

Yet, one simple change in that instruction—or code— effectively changes the outcome.

If the production team member had been more specific and said, "Bill, go get my laptop bag," instead of "Someone go get my laptop bag," we instantly improve efficiency and likely, in some immeasurable, incremental way, began to improve our outcomes. That simple change in wording alters the string of events that follow in a way that gives me better control as a manager—I now have four PAs manning their positions and one running for the bag instead of five unmanned positions—and while this may seem trivial, it's not. If the street corners that were supposed to be locked up* by any of those four PAs who are now unnecessarily running

* *Locking up* means that our perimeter is closed, so no civilians can walk into our shot when filming on location.

for a bag are compromised, it can cost us valuable shooting time. But to understand the real impact, multiply that incremental improvement by the thousands of instructions that we might issue on any given day or on any given project, and you can begin to see a clear route to higher efficiency.

Obviously, this is an incredibly simple example, and yet it demonstrates that as managers issue even mundane instructions, just as computer coders are writing code for software, we are writing code for employees. The idea is to identify the lines of code or instructions that, like "Don't call us, we'll call you," and "Bill, go get my laptop bag," instantly give you as a manager more control and have a positive and systemic structural effect on the functionality of your workforce.

Now take a look at a slightly more complex example of the Hollywood principle or inversion of control.

On the film *The Prince of Tides*, the director, Barbra Streisand, wanted a visually stunning sequence for the end of the movie that would start with the camera close on Tom Wingo (Nick Nolte) driving along a roadway during sunset outside Beaufort, South Carolina, then expand to encompass a beautiful vista of the low country. To achieve this, we would film a close shot with a tow rig,[†] which would cut to a tight helicopter shot that would widen out to a full shot of the car as the music came up and (in voiceover) Tom professed his love for Susan Lowenstein (played by Barbra). To get the aerial shot, we put a camera crew in a helicopter, and to maintain the highest degree of control and creative freedom (the chopper would be flying too low for safe execution on a live street),

---

[†] A *tow rig* is a vehicle and/or trailer used to physically tow a picture car so the actor doesn't have to drive.

we shut down roughly one mile of Route 21, the main road that connects, via the Woods Memorial Bridge, Lady's, Dataw, and St. Helena Islands to the city of Beaufort. Nick would be driving one car, and about a dozen extras would be driving "picture cars" so it would appear that there was a normal amount of traffic on our shut-down roadway as the camera crew in the helicopter filmed him from above.

Before we commenced shooting, Barbra and Stephen Goldblatt (the director of photography) had already briefed the helicopter pilot and camera operator on the intricacies of the shot from a directorial, cinematic, and creative standpoint, and Nick had received direction from Barbra about the nuances of his creative performance. The police had positioned their cruisers to block the entrance ramps to the roadway, diverting all civilian traffic, and I had assigned designated lanes to the dozen or so extras driving the picture cars, as well as the speed at which they should drive and a relative distance to keep from all the other vehicles. And they all had walkies on the seats next to them, as did Nick.

There are a number of potential risks when filming aerial shots in a sequence like this—all of which I had to assess while planning the day's work. For starters, a low-flying helicopter can be unnerving to drivers—the sound of the engine alone will make your lungs vibrate—but I deduced that since the roadway would be closed and the drivers briefed, a complication here was not probable. I also considered the possibility that a civilian driver could wander onto the road and panic at the sight of the low-flying helicopter, but I decided that this was also improbable since we had police cruisers blocking all the entrance ramps up and down the roadway. There was the chance that Nick could have an issue

while driving (also unlikely), and since the chopper would be flying extremely low as it tracked along with him, it could potentially get into trouble, too—say, if there was a mechanical problem,
a wind gust that buffeted it too close to the ground, or the blades
hit the bridge abutment—all of which I judged to be unlikely
scenarios in this case, as well. But there was one area where I
knew that things *could* go wrong and where I could preemptively
intervene: *controlling potentially confusing and distracting communication.*

In order for us to easily communicate with each other (because
we're often spread out over several hundred yards), on every film
set there are dozens of people with walkie-talkies. But once we roll
camera on a shot like this, I know that random or confusing communication can be detrimental—if not dangerous. A unique
aspect of using a walkie-talkie is that if someone is speaking, it
means he or she is pressing down the TALK button, which pre-
cludes anyone else (for example, me) from using the radio. So in
a shot like this, if someone else is talking and I have a dangerous
situation—say, I need to stop a picture car because a civilian is on
the roadway or the helicopter is too close to some high-tension
wires—I won't be able to warn them until the other person stops
talking. And those lost seconds can be life threatening. So, as I always do in these situations, I made the decision that once we were
set to go, from the time that I said, "Everybody off the air," to the
time that I yelled, "Cut!" for everyone with a walkie-talkie other
than me, barring an emergency, it was a listening device only. In
other words, I would be the only one communicating over the air
(via walkie-talkie with Nick, the drivers, the police, and, on a
two-way radio, with the chopper).

That single directive to stay off the air significantly diminished the risk involved in shooting this sequence. And it was the essence of the Hollywood principle—*I inverted control with a single command*. I effectively said, "Don't call us, I'll call you," and in so doing improved not only the safety of everyone involved but also increased the likelihood that we would get the highest-quality technical and creative performances in the most time- and cost-efficient manner.

In fact, to me—as a manager responsible for the execution of the shot, as well as its creative success and the safety of everyone involved—the benefits of making that decision were numerous. I dramatically diminished the possibility of *miscommunication*, and by eliminating what could be distracting audio communication, I increased the focus of Nick, the background drivers, chopper pilot, police, and camera crew, *and* cleared the airways for a quicker response in case there was an emergency and we needed to abort the shot.

When we were ready to go, I instructed all the background drivers to start their cars. I sent the chopper to its *first position*‡ (hovering about twenty feet above the water parallel to Nick's car), confirmed that Nick was ready, checked with Barbra, locked it up, got clearance from the police that the last civilian car had passed through on the road and that the ramps were blocked, and then yelled, "Roll it!"—which means to turn on the camera, roll sound, and slate the shot.§ When the pilot confirmed that he was ready,

---

‡ The first spot or *mark* for any actor, vehicle, prop, and the like that's in a shot.
§ All shots and takes in a movie are numbered so that during postproduction the editors can identify them.

I called, "Action!" Nick took off, the background cars began moving, the helicopter flew parallel to Nick, and the camera crew commenced filming from the low-flying chopper.

The shot went flawlessly. A few moments later, I yelled, "Cut!" The chopper landed, the camera assistant on board handed a video cassette of the footage we had just filmed to a waiting production assistant, I repositioned the cars for take two, and Barbra, Stephen, and I reviewed the tape on a monitor to see if there were adjustments to be made for the next take.

By making the simple, definitive management call to limit communication, I streamlined a complex situation and lowered the risk level for everyone involved. I also improved the likelihood of successful execution of the shot by removing cluttered, confusing communication, thereby increasing focus and concentration—and that meant that there was a better chance that we would be able to get the work in fewer takes, which kept us on schedule and on budget. And I did this with a single command that inverted control. *No radio communication other than from me.*

Now before you decide that this doesn't pertain to your line of work, consider that distracting communication is not a problem unique to film production.

Far from it.

In fact, to see just how universal this problem can be and how valuable it often is to limit stray and distracting communication, consider that virtually everyone now has a smartphone in his or her pocket. Then consider that employers rate cell phones / texting and the Internet as the largest killers of productivity.

And that distracting communication can do more than derail productivity. In May 2016, the National Transportation Safety

Board (NTSB) announced that the 2015 Amtrak crash that killed eight people and injured over two hundred outside of Philadelphia occurred because the engineer failed to reduce his speed when he was *distracted by radio communication from another train.*

WHILE THE TWO examples I just gave about the laptop bag and the aerial shot on *Prince of Tides* are examples of *individual, isolated commands* that inverted control—"Bill, go get my laptop bag" and "No one on the air but me"—what is even better is when we establish a whole system of management that has embedded structural directives that *invoke automatically* and will accomplish the same inversion of control without a verbal command at all. Using examples of how this has been done successfully in both film and non-film-related industries—from the restaurant business to ride-share companies like Uber—the following chapters will explain how to do just that.

Why is this so important? Because as managers, we want a system in place so we can achieve the outcomes we want in the most efficient way, and we want that system to *automate* and be *responsive and sensitive* so it can adapt quickly in a changing environment. In essence, what we're really striving to do is put a fluid and adaptive system of management in place so that we don't have to try so hard to be so adaptive and responsive ourselves.

What I've learned over the years is this:

If we set out as managers looking for those *beautiful lines of code that structurally and systemically change outcomes for the better,* those positive outcomes will begin to occur with little effort on our part for the simple reason that better outcomes have been built into the structure of our management directives from the onset.

And here's where it gets interesting: once I started using the core premise behind inversion of control and the Hollywood principle to manage people, time, and money, I got the same positive outcomes the coders did—a more efficient system that made my job managing large projects easier and my outcomes better. This is a compelling approach to management for a unique reason. It promises a system of project and group management that is designed to be highly efficient and highly adaptive. Therefore, for the managers employing it, and for the employees operating within it, it doesn't feel oppressive or dogmatic. Instead it's liberating, and it works. During the helicopter shot on *Prince of Tides*, no one was annoyed that they couldn't chime in on the radio. They respected that there was a manager in place making definitive decisions that facilitated a safe and successful outcome.

Once I started using the Hollywood principle, it occurred to me that it could work *for just about everything*. Not just for software architecture that employs strings of code to instruct programs to interface with users and for managers to interface with employees but also for people *in all facets of their lives* to interface with all the groups, projects, and problems they manage. And for this reason: *outcomes change, dollars are spent more efficiently, time is managed better, collaboration is maximized, innovation is stimulated, deadlines are met, stress is reduced, and conflict is diminished.*

So, as a manager, the question becomes, *how can you write strings of code—simple instructions for yourself and others—that change outcomes systemically?* Or put another way, *how do you make simple systems changes in order to create dramatic shifts in outcomes?*

The answer begins with a concept applicable to every manager in every business:

Tensile strength**
The same measurement by which the breaking point
of steel is calibrated.

Insight:

Small changes in your management approach—and even small changes in the way directives are worded—can alter outcomes significantly.

Action Steps:
Reframe the specific wording of directives to better achieve desired outcomes.
Evaluate management perspective and look to embed structural changes that will invoke better outcomes automatically.

Result:
Increased efficiency and productivity.
Less stress and conflict.
A safer workplace.

** "The resistance of a material to a force tending to tear it apart, measured as the maximum tension the material can withstand without tearing." Source: thefreedictionary.com

2

BEGIN TO BUILD TENSILE STRENGTH

★

You Have Eight Sheets of Computer Paper,
Now Go Build a Bookcase

Case Study:
The film *The Devil's Advocate.* Warner Bros. Directed by
Taylor Hackford; starring Al Pacino, Keanu Reeves, and
Charlize Theron.

When focused on building tensile strength, every single thing
you do as a team leader—every thought and every action—will
be geared toward strengthening the underlying organization in a
very goal-directed, purposeful manner. And a good leader is
aware of the maximum stress that a workforce can withstand
while being stretched or pulled before it loses structural integrity.
He or she is also aware of how to build a team with *maximum
tensile strength* so that that team can achieve peak performance as
it withstands the stresses applied by the forces of the business—
whatever that business is. In other words, as a leader you have to
engineer your team. That begins with hiring the right people—*or*
with training and managing the "wrong" people if that's the

hand you're dealt—and the upside is, thinking in terms of tensile strength impacts every facet of management going forward from there.

Once you adopt the mind-set that your goal is to build tensile strength—create the strongest team possible—it changes everything. Managers and leaders who are singularly focused on building the tensile strength of their organizations spend less time laying blame, expressing anger, suffering crippling anxiety and stress, or expending energy in other unproductive and *managerially destructive* ways. When you adopt this mind-set, it redirects your energies and changes your behavior as a manager in a fundamental way.

Consider that the concept that "a chain is only as strong as its weakest link" is often applied to managerial thinking, yet operating under this premise can *weaken* an organization—and for some very practical reasons. For starters, from a theoretical mathematical standpoint, no matter how good your team is, there will *always* be a weakest link, which means that sequentially weeding out your weakest employees will eventually leave you as a manager with a staff of one (not practical) or in a state of constant employee turnover (costly and disruptive). A high rate of turnover will likely degrade morale and create an environment where employee mistakes, and therefore risk taking, are perceived as a fast track to unemployment—a string of repercussions that erode organizational cohesion, impede creativity, and reduce the likelihood of organizational success.

Consider this management perspective instead: *The strength of a team is not dependent on the weakest link but rather is dependent on the combined tensile strength of the group.*

If you accept *this* premise, it removes the focus from your team's *individual* weaknesses and moves it to your *collective* strengths. Basing management on tensile strength presupposes that the power of the team is greater than the sum of the strengths of the individuals on that team. It also operates under the premise that individual weaknesses can be circumvented and/or compensated for. Now, that's not to suggest that managers should *always* retain weak employees but rather that there is a productive, alternative approach to framing how you *think* about the qualifications of your staff.

Team building in business isn't analogous to fantasy football; it's real life, where from a practical standpoint, most managers will never get anything approaching an actual dream team. Instead, we get a smattering of great employees and some good employees as well as some subpar employees. We get some employees we choose ourselves, and some we inherit—for any number of reasons—all of whom need to be led and managed. Rather than focusing on firing and rehiring to replace weak performers, we have the option to focus on *capitalizing and building upon the strengths of individual employees* and cultivating the collaborative efforts that will bypass and circumvent the individual weaknesses that are a given in virtually any team.*

From the standpoint of a manager, I've found that the tensile strength perspective trumps the weakest link philosophy, and adopting it can completely change your perspective about how to manage and lead. *It's one of those small coded changes that can have*

---

* Gallup reports a dramatic increase in employee engagement when managers focus on individual employee strengths rather than on their weaknesses.

a big impact. In fact, it saves precious time and money, raises morale (including your own), and cultivates organizational strength. In other words, this change in *perspective* produces both a *functional* shift (you're directing resources to build up the team you have) and a *conceptual* shift (this company is vested in its employees).

Think about this: You can build a bookshelf that is strong enough to hold a four hundred–page textbook from a few individual pieces of computer paper (or newspaper) if you know how to maximize the collective strength offered by a few flimsy sheets of paper.

(Hint: Roll an individual sheet of paper tightly to construct each leg—legs with remarkable tensile strength.)

Now apply the concept of tensile strength to a *specific* work situation.

It's Sunday morning in midtown Manhattan. I have a hundred-person film crew, A-list actors, a high-profile director, a $200,000 shooting budget—*for the day*—a permit from the mayor's office, and an elite division of "movie cops" from the NYPD to help control the streets. There are barricades set up to block roadways and sidewalks. I have a ten-story-tall Aquilla crane with a camera mounted on it standing in the middle of East Fifty-Seventh Street and an army of production assistants manning the sidewalks, storefronts, and intersections, prepared to lock up the streets and shut down this section of the city when the camera is ready to roll.

This single day of shooting on the film *Devil's Advocate* has been in planning for months. We are about to shoot the scene where Kevin Lomax (played by Keanu Reeves) exits the psych ward of a hospital after visiting his wife (played by Charlize Theron), who has just slashed her throat with a piece of broken glass. As he steps out of the hospital onto East Fifty-Seventh Street, it becomes evident that—in a fit of anger—the devil (played by Al Pacino) has just eliminated all life in New York City. When the camera cranes up, there isn't another soul to be seen. There are no pedestrians, no moving cars—no visible signs of life at all. The creative mandate for the production team was to shut down eight city blocks so that midtown Manhattan would appear to be *completely empty*. Empty like the population of Manhattan has just been vaporized—the Biblical equivalent of a neutron bomb.

To get this shot, we didn't use computer graphics to "erase" the cars and people. Instead, we actually shut down East Fifty-Seventh Street looking west toward Fifth Avenue so that it looked like the aftermath of an apocalypse. The buildings were completely intact, but the normally bustling streets of midtown Manhattan were totally devoid of humanity.

When I signaled action and the camera began rolling that day, what we needed in order to pull this off—in addition to a high level of filmmaking expertise—was an *even higher level of leadership and management skill* and a *highly functioning team*.

To get this shot, the defining element that would determine success didn't rest with the high-profile producers, the acclaimed director of photography (Andrzej Bartkowiak), the Oscar-winning director (Taylor Hackford) or the multimillion-dollar actor. Instead, at this very critical juncture, the epicenter of control rested in the hands of the production assistants locking up street corners— theoretically the weakest links in our organizational structure.[†]

[†] Note that the "weakest links" are not always the lowest-ranked employees as they happen to be in this example. In fact, they often are high-level employees.

(To flip back to my paper bookshelf analogy, *we were resting a very heavy and very expensive book on some potentially flimsy paper legs.*)

Production assistants are low-paid, entry-level film set underlings—*the least trained and experienced* of the crew. And for this scene, their job was to stop all pedestrians from walking past their assigned posts *even though technically we had no legal right to stop them from doing so.* A single pedestrian who defied the PAs and walked through the scene would have ruined our very expensive shot, and we'd have no choice but to try again to get a usable take. (On top of that, once one person decides not to cooperate and walks through the barricades, there can be a domino effect as a lot of other people follow, and we may lose control of the streets altogether.)

What this meant was that from the moment I put the call out on the walkie-talkie to "lock it up," and then moments later when I called action and the camera began rolling on that Sunday morning, those thirty-five PAs who were strategically positioned around the perimeter were the nexus of support for the entire, very expensive, shot. In order for this to work, I needed to know who I could depend on. And I needed everyone on the team to *want* to succeed.

Instead of dismissing the production assistants as "weakest links" or employees of no value, throughout the project, I let them know just how important they were in making the film from day one.

They had genuine value, and I let them know that.
Why?
Because they *do* have genuine value, and as a seasoned manager,

I know that—and by reinforcing my trust in them, it builds their confidence in their ability to do the job.

And practicing management concretely based on the Hollywood principle means that you are employing systems theory.

Consider a car. Every single part of an automobile has a defined function. The rearview mirror serves a distinct function from the carburetor and the windshield wipers. The gas tank has a different function than the steering wheel. They operate individually to accomplish specific tasks that collectively accomplish something that none of the individual parts can do alone. *Even though each part has discrete functionality, in concert, they function as a system.*

As a seasoned manager, I know that even a failure of the tiniest, seemingly most insignificant part can make a car (a relatively simple mechanical system)—let alone a film set (a far more complex open system impacted by numerous external forces)—inoperable. That is, of course, the foundation of systems theory. And what, after all, is your organization attempting to become? *A functioning system that has more strength and higher output than any of the component parts could generate separately.* But how do you find, hire, train, and trust people to build the kind of organizational tensile strength that you can rely on in a situation like the one I just described on *Devil's Advocate*?

For starters, since I am always *thinking* in terms of tensile strength, I was planning for that shot from the first day I read the script—and building a team that would have the organizational strength to pull it off from day one. And since every film has at least one nearly impossible sequence, I keep *that* scene—or scenes—top of mind when I hire and train staff, as well as when

I assess the skills, work ethic, speed, technical proficiency, reliability, and even the personalities of the entire cast and crew.

So the questions become:

> How do you shift from thinking about individual weaknesses to concentrating on the collective strengths of employees?

> And how do you build enough tensile strength in your organization so that you can maintain total control when the stakes are incredibly high and as a team manager you have no choice at critical times but to rely on team members who may be less than perfect?

> In other words, how do you roll thin pieces of paper so tightly that they can hold an extraordinary amount of weight?

It starts with creating highly segmented and discrete jobs[‡] and establishing open and fluid communication, which circles back to why filmmaking is such a good example for management, leadership, and team building.

First, the job categories in film production are *highly special-*

[‡] The relationship between job segmentation and increased productivity is of course what fueled the Industrial Revolution, and job segmentation has been written about by scholars as far back as Plato, by Adam Smith in *An Inquiry into the Nature and Causes of the Wealth of Nations*, and Émile Durkheim in *The Division of Labour in Society*. Others like Henry David Thoreau, Karl Marx, and Alexis de Tocqueville worried about job specialization causing a disconnect between workers and the end process. What I will be discussing in this book is a very fine-tuned form of job specialization that works to increase productivity as it simultaneously elevates the individual workers' sense of connection to the group and to the project as a whole.

ized to begin with, so there is little room for actual competition on set. *This is an absolutely critical component in building a team with tensile strength.*

With little or no *direct competition*, this structure creates a strong sense of *personal responsibility*. Think about that scene I just described from *Devil's Advocate*. The job of the PAs was *so segmented* that the only thing they each had to do was control the pedestrian traffic from *that one spot they were assigned to*. When I gave each PA a specific location to lock up, all of them knew *exactly* what they had to do and that they were personally responsible for that sidewalk/corner/shop. That kind of segmented responsibility creates *accountability and pride*.

This type of very specific task segmentation in filmmaking is not unique to the production staff. In film production, there are numerous departments (camera, transportation, art, set decoration, props, electric, etc.) and hierarchies within those departments, and the work is so segmented and so clearly delineated that the atmosphere is one that promotes *individual accountability as a means to achieve collective success*. What this does for individual workers between and within departments is that to a large degree it changes the focus from thinking about how *I* can succeed *for me* to how can *we* succeed as a team *for us*, and from what can *I* slough off to someone else to what I *have to do* as a member of a team for the collective good of the project. To consider just how broad the application of this can be, think of a floor littered with red and blue blocks in a kindergarten classroom. If the teacher just says to the whole class, "Go clean up the blocks," there is no individual accountability, and because of that, there is a good chance that the job won't get done. If instead, he or she rewrites the code—or instruction—and one specific child is tasked with picking up all the red blocks and another is tasked with picking up all the blue blocks, there is no *competition* during the process of picking up blocks, and yet there is *enormous individual accountability*. We will all know who didn't do his or her job by the color of the blocks left on the floor. *And that reality functions to motivate and change outcomes.*

Of course, this concept has applications far beyond a kindergarten classroom. When the American Marketing Association (AMA) examined the differences between high-performance and low-performance organizations (based on comparisons of revenue growth, market share, profitability, and customer satisfaction), they found that two drivers of high performance were *consistency* and *clarity*. And job segmentation delivers both. When looking at what separated employees at high- and low-performance companies, the Boston Consulting Group found that those at the high-performance companies, "know what they are supposed to be doing and how that relates to the tasks of their neighbors." In other words, *clear strategy and concise goals lead to high performance.*

To show just how highly segmented our jobs are on a film set, and how well that functions to create organizational success, consider this actual (common) event: we are shooting a scene in a kitchen and a lightbulb over the kitchen table has to be replaced.

Yet not just anyone can change the lightbulb.

In order to accomplish this simple task, *a half dozen departments have to be involved.*

First, a propman has to remove all the props on the table—dishes, tablecloth, silverware, books, wineglasses, centerpiece, and the like.[§] Next, a couple of set dressers step in to move the kitchen table. (The set dressers are the only ones permitted by union rules to handle furniture—or set dressing—when we shoot.) Then a grip (third department involved) brings in a ladder and sets it up under the fixture and removes any diffusion in front of the light. Next, an electrician (the fourth union person involved) climbs the ladder and changes the lightbulb. He/she steps off the ladder, and the grip climbs back up to replace the diffusion and then removes the ladder. The set dressers bring the table back in, and the property man resets the props (dishes, tablecloth, silverware, books, wineglass, vase, etc.). The camera assistant (fifth union person) redoes the focus marks, and, *finally* we've changed the lightbulb. And all of this is being overseen by someone like me who is a member of the Directors Guild and a sixth department—production.

Sounds idiotic and expensive, right?

Wrong.

If the props (dishes, tablecloth, etc.) aren't put back *exactly* where they were before the light blew, then any coverage we shoot going forward for this scene won't match what we previously shot. In other words, if the props are set in the wrong place after the lightbulb is changed, in subsequent shots, the wineglass, centerpiece, and other props may "jump" two feet over, the plate may be off center, and the book open to a different page—so the footage wouldn't match for continuity when it is cut together in the editing room and would be unusable. (The prop department

---

[§] A *prop* can refer to someone in the property department or to an actual physical item used in the shot like sunglasses, a coffee cup, a gun, and so on.

photographs and marks the table so they know exactly where to put everything back in place.) This need for meticulous precision mandates that no one other than a propman can touch the props because once they have been established in a shot, they have to be put back in *precisely* the same positions. As for the electricians changing the lightbulb, there's a reason for that, too. Since we often work with high voltage, this is a safety precaution that dictates that "all things to do with electricity" have to be handled by a qualified electrician. So while this may *look and sound* petty and uneconomical to a layperson, it is a safety measure that *saves rather than wastes money*—and it sometimes even saves lives.

Yet that is only the *filmmaking* side of the lightbulb-changing equation. From a *management perspective*, when everyone knows by union contract exactly what they are *allowed to do*, it completely diminishes any infighting over *who should do what*.

This creates departmental importance and individual pride in work.

It also spawns industry jokes like these:

How many actors does it take to change a lightbulb?

Fifteen. One to change the bulb and fourteen to say, "I could have done that."

How many teamsters does it take to change a lightbulb?

Twenty. You got some kind of a fuckin' problem with that?

How many producers does it take to change a lightbulb?

Five. One to hold the bulb and four to rotate the chair.

And of course, what is really ironic is that none of those people would ever be allowed to change a lightbulb on a film set in the first place.

But here's where it gets really interesting. *What I just described is an industry that has jobs that are highly segmented and departments that are—theoretically—siloed.* Of course, silos on farms are cylindrical towers used to store grain, but in business, silos are metaphorical cylindrical towers that isolate people and tasks. In most businesses, silos are a natural offshoot of company growth, discrete departments, and regional offices. However, as much as silos in business allow for specialization (sales, marketing, design . . .) in a *productive way*, they also can undermine success and profit for some very obvious reasons.

A big concern in business today is that siloed departments often foster siloed agendas, which foster siloed outcomes through a complex web that often begins with geographic- and knowledge-based isolation and leads to institutionalized interdepartmental competition and a lack of organizational cohesion. If the sales department is siloed, they may not *really be* interested in what the marketing department is doing. And marketing may not talk to—or respect—sales *or* the design teams. This can create environments where employees feel not so much that they're part of a corporate team but that they are pegged against other employees in other divisions in a *let's see who can win at all costs in a micro-interdepartmental-level* competition, where all thoughts of a corporate-wide *we're in this together with a common goal* mentality have flown out the window. Talk to any corporate managers and you'll likely find that if they are head of a division, they are trying to put up numbers that will trump every other division. It's corporate and human nature. The paradox is that while silos dominate the corporate landscape and are functional and necessary, there is widespread frustration that at the same time they undermine broad-based, overall corporate success. Behnam Tabrizi reported in June 2015 in *Harvard Business Review* that when he looked at ninety-five teams at twenty-five major corporations "nearly 75% of cross-functional** teams are dysfunctional." Which means that when these siloed departments are assembled into teams to work together, they are ineffective. He defined dysfunction as failing at three or more of the following criteria: staying on budget, meeting scheduled deadlines, adhering to specs, and meeting customer and/or corporate goals. Tabrizi attributes all the failures to *poor management*—unclear governance, a lack of accountability, poorly specified goals, and failure to prioritize projects across teams.

Yet in film production—an industry that has extremely siloed departments based on specialized skill sets and highly discrete jobs—when we work together there is admirable cohesion, unification of purpose, the highest possible creative output, and enviable intra- and interdepartmental teamwork. Why do we manage to be successful using a system that seems to fail for so many companies? Why don't we get the unhealthy competition—that departmental "isolationism" and "nationalism" that can define the culture within many organizations? Just as Tabrizi identified, it comes down to *the way those silos are managed*: with *good management*—clear governance, total accountability, patently specified goals, and prioritization of projects across teams.

So what is it *specifically* about film production—an industry that has siloed structure but un-siloed results—that allows us to do that?

** *Cross-functional* teams are teams comprised of people from different (siloed) departments. On a film set when we move from preproduction to shooting, we are essentially creating a large cross-functional team from our smaller siloed departments.

For starters, we have a large crew of people in siloed departments *working to create a single product* rather than a small group separated from the larger group and assigned the task of working to create single products or solutions that will only be *one part* of a long list of products or solutions for that company. And while most companies can't replicate the single-product model, what we are *really* doing is structuring a system where every single employee and department is connected to a *single final goal*. That, in and of itself, is *a coded way* to prevent the downside effects of siloed departments. But how *exactly* does it work?

THE FIRST ELEMENT IS *WORKPLACE GEOGRAPHY*.

On set, we practically trip over each other when we are shooting. That creates a sense of *solidarity* and *common purpose*. It also facilitates the natural flow of *communication and the development of mutual respect*. Everyone on the crew sees the hard work of the electricians hauling cable, the set dressers moving furniture, and scenic artists painting, and everyone is working in concert as the director of photography, director, and actors do *their* jobs, which will ultimately enable us to *collectively* get that shot and *collectively move as a team* on to the next shot or scene on our schedule. The driver of that cohesion is the fact that we are sequestered together in a physical workplace that is perceptually, at least, a level playing field, *and* we are working toward a *single common goal*. And that means that the success of each department is codependent on the success of every other department—*and we are constantly made aware of that fact.*

A film with stunning photography and brilliant makeup will

probably not get recognized as a great film artistically or commercially if the actors' performances are poor, the direction is weak, or the quality of the sound recording is flawed, no matter how good the camerawork or makeup might look. Further, we can't move on to the next shot on the schedule until we get the shot we are currently working on. That means forward motion is dependent on every department succeeding in an orchestrated effort.

Many companies create siloed departments to silo expertise but then fail to structure those silos in a way that renders them part of a larger team with a common goal and in a way that organically creates mutual respect for the work of other team members. Instead, they are often siloed in different parts of the building—or even in different cities and countries—structured with isolated departments with department-specific goals. Exacerbating the situation even more is the fact that those departments often post competing success metrics, which is often more conducive to *competition* than it is to *cooperation*.

Now many companies can't—and shouldn't—work in such close quarters, but there are numerous ways of replicating the positive outcome of *proximity* in ways that don't feel forced. Companies such as Facebook, Google, and Apple understand the value of cross-departmental interface and have purposefully reconfigured their workplaces so people from siloed departments will be, effectively, *forced* to interact with a high degree of frequency and do so in less formal situations—say, by bumping into each other as they walk in and out of buildings or go to restrooms and other common spaces that have been laid out specifically so employees from different departments will have opportunities to interact and exchange information.

I intentionally alter the geography of our workplace in pre-production (when we are in offices and not working in the confined space of a film set) in two simple, specific ways. First, I make it a point to float around with a cup of coffee in the morning and pop into individual offices—say, the production designer, wardrobe designer, cinematographer, or director—just to say good morning. *Remember, these are often people I have never worked with before.* This is a casual way to get to know and assess people and allows me to address issues in a very informal manner, thereby increasing information flow. *It also communicates that as a manager, I am accessible.* Second, I institute an informal Monday morning department head meeting to get an update on where we are, see who needs help, and field questions. *This is presented as "I am here to help" rather than "I am checking up on you,"* and it increases interdepartmental communication in a manner that allows what are very siloed departments working independently to interact. This improves communication, prevents problems from developing in the first place, and facilitates early intervention for the problems that have arisen. As simple and small as they are, both of these efforts build relationships, increase comfort levels, and provide support in nonthreatening and unintimidating ways— in other words, they build the tensile strength of our team.

There are numerous other creative ways to play with workplace geography that don't involve moving walls or working on top of one another. Consider how companies that offer royalties to employees—say, chemical/food/flavor companies that develop formulas—can manipulate pay structure to, in effect, alter the geography of the workplace, as well. For example, if they pay a full royalty to *all* employees who contribute to a formula regardless of the size of that contribution (rather than paying a pro rata share), they bring everyone closer together by creating an environment where it *literally* pays to collaborate. That pay structure will increase information sharing and teamwork, diminish competition, and establish a common goal. This is costlier in the short run—the company may have to pay a full royalty to several contributing employees rather than to only one—but management has ensured collaboration and probably a better product, and therefore likely higher revenue, since under this pay structure no one has a financially vested interest in developing a formula completely on his or her own. And that single change in royalty pay structure effectively changes the workplace geography by changing the frequency and quality of the interactions of employees who are now far more interested in the work of their colleagues and are incentivized to seek it out. This in turn increases communication and information sharing as it builds the tensile strength of the company and improves the quality of what is being produced; and it does so in a way that will continue to occur with no additional effort on the part of management. It's a small coded change that *automates* better outcomes.

Beyond workplace geography and the maintenance of a common goal, how *else* is the managerial structure of film production set up to facilitate this high level of cohesion on such large projects with siloed departments and segmented jobs?

We have a *KEYSTONE MANAGER* in place.

The Romans began using keystones to support arches when they understood that a designated stone set at the peak of an arch—a keystone—provides crucial stability because it redistributes the weight down the columns of the arch. If you take the keystone out, the arch falls. In the case of a company composed of siloed departments, the keystone role is played by a manager *who has power over those silos* and—this is critical—*no skewed, self-serving personal agenda because his or her job is structured so he or she doesn't have one.* In my case, I am managing individuals and department heads with differing and sometimes conflicting interests—at least in the short term. The director wants more takes or another shot, even if it means overtime. The cinematographer wants more time to light. The producer wants to wrap and stay within budget. I can be objective so they all get what is best for the project as a whole. I fight for the director and cinematographer when the shot or lighting time is necessary and side with the producer when it's not. A keystone manager is objective; he or she is someone who can balance the needs of individuals and individual departments against the collective needs of the group and the project as a whole in an unbiased manner. In other words, a keystone manager is someone whose job, responsibility, and authority is structured in a way that he or she is in a position *to be the "conscience" of the project.*

A board of directors is often considered to be the conscience of a company. But in filmmaking, our $50–100 million, one-product company doesn't have one of those. As a leader and manager, my job is designed so that I can be the *conscience* of the film, and it's a perspective that simplifies virtually every decision I have to make. The director and the producer can end up at odds—one is stewarding the art and the other has supreme control over the money—so when I explain to them that my job is to be the conscience of the film, it is my way of informing them that I understand their *individual* concerns and that I am there to serve the needs of both of them by being the voice of objective reason.

In other words, keystone managers increase the tensile strength of an organization because they have both *objectivity* and the *authority to act*. Therefore, they are in a position to make unbiased decisions that serve the whole rather than the individual.

And that brings us back to the Hollywood principle. Just like with the saying "Don't call us, we'll call you," the route to transformational change can be simple if it's both *structural* and *systemic*. By maintaining a common goal, superimposing interdepartmental proximity, and putting a keystone manager in place who has power over those silos and whose only goal is the success of the project as a whole, you are writing lines of managerial code that will transform what are often isolating, competitive, and fractional (but necessary) skill-based silos into silos of expertise and functionality that are highly productive and cohesive.

But beyond clearly segmenting jobs and delineated responsibility,[††] considering workplace geography, maintaining a common goal, and inserting a keystone manager, what other steps can you take to augment the process of building tensile

---

[††] Note that I work with a large staff and many backup options. Small operations need to have contingency plans in place to guard against having jobs so segmented that if one employee is sick or quits no one else can do that work. In small companies, managers have to be careful to segment individual *assignments*, not necessarily *jobs*. We, like most large companies, are positioned to always have backup personnel available, especially for critical tasks.

strength, and what else can you do as a manager to execute a high level of functionality in your workplace?

ESTABLISH CLEAR LINES OF COMMUNICATION. (THOSE COMPONENT PARTS WITH DISCRETE FUNCTIONALITY HAVE TO COMMUNICATE WITH EACH OTHER.)

On a film set, since I am the *keystone manager* and all inter-departmental communication flows through me, I am able to maintain an environment where cohesion and cooperation are king. No department feels isolated from the rest—or less important, because there is someone in place who is designated to address and coordinate their needs. And as for my own department—production—with the exception of dangerous shots and stunts where I take tight control of the airways and communication flow, I am in constant communication with them either in person or by walkie-talkie at all times. And in turn, they are in constant communication with each other as well—which means they feel supported and not alone, even when they *are alone—say, when standing two blocks away from the camera, locking up a street corner.*

There is hard evidence to support just how important communication is and why it is critical in improving employee performance—even weaker employees' performance—and therefore in changing the tensile strength of those "weak links" and compensating for any inherent organizational deficits. At the Massachusetts Institute of Technology (MIT) Human Dynamics Laboratory, researchers looking at why some call center teams at a bank outperformed others found that differences in *communication* explained widely differing performance among what seemed to be identical teams and that the teams' *energy* and *engagement* outside formal meetings were the best predictors of productivity. The researchers found that these factors explained "one-third of the variations in dollar productivity among groups." In fact, what they found was that "patterns of communication" affected performance *more than any other variable*. In order to improve performance, instead of firing the weakest performing call center employees, the bank *manipulated workplace geography* (think Facebook, Google, and Apple and what I do in preproduction) and created opportunities to increase informal communication by changing the weaker call center employee coffee break schedules to coincide with the stronger call center employees break times—therefore giving the weaker employees more face time with stronger employees. That single shift improved performance of the weak call center employees—which the bank estimated would translate to a $15 million increase in productivity—*not because they fired the weakest performers or rebuilt their headquarters but because they manipulated the workplace geography by simply changing break schedules as a means to improve communication. And by making a small change in the way they led and managed those "weak" employees, they were able to alter outcomes for the better.*‡‡

Consider again the geography of a film set. If we're filming on a soundstage, we're in an open environment with people from all departments working side by side. If it's at an interior location—

‡‡ By intermingling weak and strong performers, those coffee breaks offered valuable, informal training—weaker employees could ask questions and get advice from stronger coworkers in nonthreatening, organic, impromptu situations—and it also provided opportunities to increase a sense of cohesion and common purpose.

say, an apartment, office, or restaurant—it can be big or small, but again, we're all pooled together—sometimes working in close quarters and on top of one another. If we're at an exterior location—say, a city street or on a beach—we may be spread out, but we then use walkie-talkies to communicate. That maintains constant, fluid conversation up, down, and across all departments. We don't have walls—literal or figurative. And that geographic structure allows free-flowing information. But here is the key: there is a defined system of information flow up, through, and between departments. Department underlings communicate to department heads. Department heads communicate information to me. I disseminate to other department heads as necessary—in other words, we are highly organized, and there is little opportunity for chaos. It's an elaborate structure that allows for free-flowing communication that is managed through a fine-tuned and purposeful system with an assigned *keystone manager* in control. It may look like mayhem when we are filming, but there's structure to the way we transmit and delineate information. *Critical structure. And that builds organizational cohesion as it prevents individuals from making uninformed, detrimental decisions. At the same time, it also instills confidence in employees that the project has a leader and that every single department's concerns are being heard and addressed.*

Now, think of *your* specific company or organization. Consider if segmenting jobs to remove direct competition will create an environment that is conducive to a higher level of both job satisfaction and productive collaboration at your company.

Then ask yourself this:

How can I create segmented jobs where there is no direct competition between the performance of one employee and another; one where ownership of a specific task leads to responsibility, accountability, and pride in the individual employees performing that task?

Can I create greater interdepartmental cooperation and respect by removing walls—literally and figuratively?

Can I structure—and emphasize—a common goal for the entire company?

Do I have a keystone manager in place who is an empowered decision-maker whose job and responsibilities are structured in a way that he or she has no personal agenda other than the success of the project as a whole, and who is in control of information flow?

And then:

How else can I improve communication to improve functionality? And can I open up communication both *vertically* and *horizontally* while still maintaining control?

Vertical communication (low-level employees communicating with middle- and high-level employees) is not only critical for training but also makes employees feel valued, while horizontal communication (between people with similar jobs) makes employees feel supported—two factors that lead to highly functioning teams.

Bear in mind that this is not window dressing—when it's coded into the system, it's management and leadership *that works*.

Creating segmented jobs and discrete tasks and coupling that with fluid communication facilitated by frequent cross-departmental contact overseen by a keystone manager is an effective way for employees to improve performance and is the first step in building an organization with increased tensile strength.

There is an added benefit to this type of management, as well: numerous studies of military personnel have demonstrated that the more cohesive a unit feels, the lower the levels of post-traumatic stress disorder (PTSD). *We're talking about the improved psychological health of your employees. In jobs with high stress and tough working conditions, this is very important to keep in mind.*

Now think about what an increase in tensile strength and a feeling of cohesion would do for your workforce and how that might generate higher profits, greater innovation and job satisfaction, and make *your* job as a manager easier. Then stop thinking about the individual weaknesses of your team and start thinking in terms of building tensile strength by removing your focus from those *individual weaknesses* and moving it to *collective strengths* while *focusing on job segmentation; workplace geography; making sure that you have—or are yourself—a keystone manager who has a position of power, is the "conscience" of the project, and is a conduit for fluid communication.*

INSIGHT:

Focusing on collective team strength rather than on individual weaknesses paves the way to build stronger teams as it changes management perspective in a constructive manner.

Action Steps:

Focus on building team strength.

Create segmented jobs and discrete tasks.

Consider creative ways to manipulate workplace geography to increase contact, cooperation, respect, and information flow.

Set common goals.

Structure a position of a keystone manager who functions without a personal agenda or bias.

Result:

More cohesive workforce.

Fewer siloed outcomes.

Better communication flow.

Less workplace tension.

Improved efficiency and a more content workforce.

Greater chance of overall success.

3

ENGINEER EPIC TRUST

★

Everest Style

Case Study:
The film *F/X*. Orion Pictures. Directed by Robert Mandel;
starring Bryan Brown, Brian Dennehy, and Diane Venora.

By detailing the crane shot from *Devil's Advocate* in chapter 2,
I illustrated how creating segmented jobs, assigning discrete tasks,
adopting an overall management style that genuinely values the
contributions of individual employees, and putting a keystone
manager in place who is the conscience of the project and a conduit
for establishing clear lines of communication are the foundation
for building tensile strength. And this, in turn, leads to accountability, pride in work, tight control, and high productivity.

But consider that in that example from *Devil's Advocate*, if the
production assistants hadn't done their jobs well and we had lost
control of the streets, at worst, we wouldn't have gotten the shot.
As costly as that would have been to our budget, the damage would
have been contained to that; *our project wouldn't have been ruined,*

and nobody would have died. Since the need for, and the value of, a high level of organizational strength increases as the stakes go up, it begs the question, *what else can I do as a manager to increase the tensile strength of my team so that when I face even bigger challenges and tackle increasingly complex tasks I have the best chance of success?*

The next essential component in tensile strength building involves slowly and incrementally establishing *bilateral trust*—that is, trust of employees in management and, conversely, trust of management in those employees.

IN THE OPENING sequence of the film *F/X*, a hit man carrying a machine gun enters a crowded restaurant and opens fire. A waiter serving a flambé dessert is shot, and when he's hit, the flaming dessert lands on a diner whose clothes burst into flames. Within seconds, he becomes a human torch, burning from head to toe. As the hit man continues to shoot and patrons run for cover, a bartender is sprayed with bullets, the mirror behind the bar is blown to pieces, and three, one-thousand-gallon lobster tanks explode, sending water and lobsters cascading onto the floor.

There were numerous component parts to this stunt sequence, the toughest of which was lighting a man on fire. To do this, we didn't use computer graphics, and we didn't just light his sleeve or pant leg on fire. Rather, this was a *full-body burn* that literally involved dressing the stuntman in fire-retardant clothing and wig, coating all his exposed skin (everything but his eyes, which were left unprotected) with a nonflammable, protective gel, and then covering him with an accelerant and igniting it. It was a dangerous and technical challenge that could have ended with serious injury or even the loss of life. It required complex choreography, tight control and technical expertise, weeks of meticulous planning, the implementation of extreme safety measures, enormous discipline, and total focus from everyone involved. That and *deep-seated bilateral trust.*

Managers in a situation where the stakes are *this* high have to have trust in every member of their workforce and be certain that each of them has the skill and confidence to pull off something of this magnitude.

At the same time, those employees involved in executing and performing a stunt like this have to trust that their manager is in total control at all times and will protect *them* so they will have the confidence *they* need to do *their* jobs well.

It's worth noting that from a manager's perspective, in addition to the escalating danger, there is a second key difference between this example and the one from *Devil's Advocate*; the PAs I had to manage for the scene where we shut down midtown Manhattan were only being tasked with holding back pedestrian traffic. Although this was critical for the shot, *it required minimal skill.* But to execute a stunt like a full-body burn—since I run and am responsible for everything on set at all times—I had to manage employees who were highly trained experts, each in a uniquely specialized, technical area, and I had to do so even though I didn't have the same training and expertise that they did. *This gap in technical knowledge and expertise is very common between managers and employees, and, as counterintuitive as it may seem, it is well documented that the best managers are often those who don't have a high level of technical expertise in the* *field*—a fact that makes building that mutual trust both more important and more difficult.*

The question is, as a manager, how do you even *start* to build that level of trust—especially in situations where there is not only a lot at stake but there are also gaps in knowledge and skill between manager and employees?

FIRST, CONSIDER *WHO* IS INVOLVED AND THEIR SKILL LEVELS—BECAUSE THAT WILL FRAME *HOW* YOU BUILD THE TRUST.

For the full-body burn in *F/X*, in addition to our regular crew, we utilized a professional stunt coordinator who hired the stuntmen and stuntwomen we needed and who also worked with us to choreograph and perform the "gag."[†] In this case, that stunt coordinator, Frank Ferrara, played the role of the diner we lit on fire. We also hired a special effects team (SFX men), led by Connie Brink, whose job it was to set up all the physical elements necessary to perform the stunt. They're the guys who apply the fire-repellant gel to the stuntman's skin, rig the explosives, set up squibs (gunpowder charges) for the bullet hits around the room, and are responsible for extinguishing the fire when we cut—or if something were to go wrong.[‡]

---

* In other words, their expertise and skill set is in *management*. For example, I am called on to manage dangerous stunts even though I am not a trained stuntman. Like most managers, my expertise and skill set is first and foremost in *management*. See Google Project Oxygen study for more information.
[†] Most of the restaurant patrons and staff were stuntmen and stuntwomen— not extras—because of the dangerous nature of what we were doing.
[‡] We don't actually use live ammunition in the guns. Instead, blanks are fired, and charges are set in specified locations to replicate bullet hits.

SECOND, CONSIDER *WHAT* IS INVOLVED, BECAUSE BUILDING TRUST IS CONTINGENT ON *WHAT YOU ARE DOING*, *HOW MUCH IS AT RISK*, AND *HOW WELL YOU LAY OUT YOUR PLAN*.

Obviously, it is during the planning stages of any project that the seeds of trust are established, and it is here that you as a manager can make everyone involved feel confident that you are doing everything possible to support and protect them and everything possible to make this tough task as easy—and safe—as it can be. For example, in the full-body burn in *F/X*, we carefully planned and choreographed each individual element of the stunt considering director Bob Mandel's aesthetic vision for how he wanted the scene to look, the technical limitations of what could be done, and the budget and safety constraints. Toward those ends, we designed and built a restaurant set on a soundstage (the sequence was too big, too complex, too dangerous, and too destructive to shoot in a real restaurant). But more important, building the set allowed us *total control*; for example, walls were moveable and built with flame-retardant material and could quickly be replaced with duplicate walls if necessary for additional takes.

As is standard in dangerous and expensive shots, we ran multiple cameras to simultaneously cover different points of view and improve the chances that we would get the coverage we needed in a single take. Even still, if the actors didn't hit their marks or missed a line, if the squibs didn't go off, or any number of other potential "failures" occurred, we'd have to do the shot again. That could cost us up to half a day, and we'd potentially be putting lives at risk for a second time. If take two *was* necessary (and in this case, for the exploding lobster tanks, it was), we'd also have to rebuild the room. We had to set up the new lobster tanks rigged for bullet hits, clean up the water, and redress. All the actors and stuntmen had to go through makeup, hair, and wardrobe again. All in, take two of the cascading lobsters required a costly two- to three-hour cleanup and redress.

But if we had to do take two for the full-fire burn (we didn't) we'd have to reset and reprep the stuntman, which would require the same lengthy redress we had for the lobster tanks—but in this case, we'd also have to light him on fire a *second time*, and no stuntman wants to be lit on fire more than once because something mundane went wrong.§

AFTER YOU OBJECTIVELY ASSESS *WHO* YOU NEED TO RELY ON AND *WHAT* THEY NEED TO DO, YOU THEN HIRE THE BEST TEAM POSSIBLE.

By the time I was overseeing this stunt on *F/X*, I had been working in the business for a long time and knew the top stunt coordinators in the industry very well, so experience and reputation—theirs and mine—played a key part in the mutual trust-building we needed to pull this off.

JUST AS OUTLINED IN CHAPTER 1, *COMMUNICATION* PLAYS AN IMPORTANT ROLE HERE, AS WELL.

In a scene as dangerous and complex as this, rather than disseminating information on a need-to-know basis as I usually do in

---

§ Stuntmen do get extra pay for each additional take due to the danger and risk involved, and they often want to do additional takes for the chance to earn more money or execute a better performance, but usually not for something this dangerous.

my management role, I tell everyone that I *really* want to know what they are thinking about *for every aspect of the stunt,* beginning on day one of the planning stages and right up to the point where we roll camera and we do the shot. I want to know every single concern, every challenge, problem, and worry—no matter how trivial they might seem. I want to hear every time or dollar issue and any crazy what-ifs. *I make it clear that this isn't a place to hold back a question or concern.* This style of *open-forum communication* is another significant element that works to build trust and confidence between managers and employees working in extreme conditions, and I make sure that the team knows that I greatly value their opinions.

> IT'S ALSO IMPORTANT FOR A MANAGER TO
> UNDERSTAND THAT IN A SITUATION WITH A HIGH
> LEVEL OF INHERENT RISK, NO ONE WILL TRUST YOU
> TO LEAD JUST BECAUSE YOU HAVE A TITLE AND ARE
> "THE BOSS."

In other words, you might be the *assigned leader,* but you must also be perceived as the *emergent leader as well*—that is, someone who garners allegiance from the workforce because of genuine respect—not job title.** In my case, that means that I schedule a stunt of this magnitude at the back end of the project—that way, there's time for relationships and trust to develop, as well as for any "untrustworthy" employees to be identified. Also, I don't

---

** Being aware of this, I always establish myself as trustworthy even though I have the authority and job title that technically makes it unnecessary. I am also always on the lookout for emergent leaders within each department who have the respect of the crew but not necessarily title or seniority, because these are often the individuals to go to when you want something done.

bookend a stunt like this between anything too demanding, either, so we don't go into it too fatigued. And, of course, we also rehearse numerous times without the fire or explosions to get the mechanics and choreography right for each department and each individual involved.

At this point, you might be thinking that this high level of mutual trust I am striving for would be nice to have but is unnecessary in your business because it doesn't really apply—after all, you don't blow up buildings or light people on fire. Yet if you look at the statistics on trust in the workplace, you'll see that employee-manager trust affects *performance and profit* in quantifiable ways, *regardless of workplace danger.*

Consider this:

A full 82 percent of workers feel that trust in superiors is essential to performance, yet 60 percent report that they don't have a high level of trust in their superiors.

Think about that—something that employees report *is essential for performance* isn't being delivered by a majority of supervisors.

Here's how that manifests:

Companies with the highest level of employee trust in managers are *two and a half times more likely* to lead in revenue growth when compared to companies that have the lowest levels of employee trust in their supervisors.

In yet another study, this one conducted by *Harvard Business Review* of twenty thousand workers around the world, *respect* was identified as a key factor in *focus, satisfaction at work, retention*, and *employee engagement*. And we know how critical employee engagement is for a company's success. I reported earlier that employee *disengagement* is a driver of both revenue loss *and* business failure.[††] And remember, this data is based on people in far more "normal" jobs than mine that don't likely involve explosions, gunfire, lighting those employees on fire, or other high-risk situations.

But even if you acknowledge the importance of bilateral trust, you could argue that so far all this advice I've given, while important, seems relatively *obvious*.

Clearly, in order to build the level of trust and respect I am talking about, a manager has to go beyond the obvious steps of assessing who and what, hiring top people, establishing open communication, and scheduling a tough assignment in a manner that allows mutual trust to develop. Over the years, I've isolated *two very specific strategies* we employ in filmmaking that work very effectively to build the highest levels of bilateral trust, and the beauty is that they can be used by *any* manager to successfully accomplish virtually *any* daunting task. And these strategies are both iterations of the job segmentation described in chapter 2.

The first involves *fractional scheduling*—breaking down each

---

[††] As mentioned in the introduction, Gallup estimates that low employee engagement accounts for 70 percent of the US workforce and costs businesses in the vicinity of $500 billion a year in lost revenue. Companies with above-average employee engagement had twice the likelihood of success as those with below-average employee engagement, and those in the ninety-ninth percentile of employee engagement had quadruple the success rate.

piece of the day's work (in this example, the stunt) into tiny, incremental, and executable component parts.

For example, as we do with all scenes, this stunt sequence in *F/X* was first broken down into a number of shots. We shot the full-body burn separately from the lobster tanks exploding, which was a separate shot from the bartender getting hit, and so forth. On top of that, each incremental segment of each of those shots was then broken down into *its* incremental, component parts.

The second element involves breaking down *those* steps *for each individual employee into incremental component parts, as well.*

As a single example, we choreograph the movement of each and every actor—and each department member—in a stunt down to the most minute detail. The premise behind this practice is based on the fact that even though the overall execution of a stunt like this may present as overwhelming, most everyone will feel confident enough to agree on how to execute each fractional step— say, for example, that we will set *exactly* seventeen squibs in the far wall in *precisely predetermined places*, and the stuntman, once ignited, will stand for *exactly* three seconds—*not two seconds, and not four*—before running off camera on *a very specific agreed-upon path*. And that's just how detailed and exacting we get. As a manager, I have learned that intentionally and systematically breaking the day's work into tiny, fractional pieces provides structure and direction, reduces stress, increases focus, and creates a sequence of controlled, executable steps that help build the type of bilateral, epic trust you need to pull off tasks of enormous scope. The fact that everyone on the cast and crew knows that this microscopic dissection of tasks is coded into everything we do gives them confidence from the onset that whatever we do will be highly managed and well executed.

Dissecting the overall task into fragments and then further dissecting those fragments into *their* component parts for each employee, and essentially mapping out the steps for them, has myriad functional and conceptual benefits. *What this means is that, in filmmaking, we not only segment jobs but we also segment time and tasks, effectively taking control of overwhelming assignments by tackling them incrementally.* And this has a staggering and positive impact on the functionality of the team and the mutual trust we have to build in order to succeed.

What's most interesting is that we don't do this just for stunts. Our fractional scheduling is so coded into the process of film production that it begins at the very onset of every project. Even before the crew is hired and the locations are found or the production office is set up, I break the script down, which is the first step in our fractional scheduling and is a process of numbering each individual scene, moving consecutively from the first word in the script to the last. In a 110-page script, we may have two hundred or more scenes, and once numbered I then create what are called breakdown sheets where key information for that scene is noted—*is it interior or exterior? Day or night? Which actors are in the scene? What is the location? What props are required?*

Next, that information is transposed—either by hand or computer—from those breakdown sheets onto thin color-coded strips created specifically for this purpose. To schedule the film in preproduction, once all the strips are made, I begin to assemble them into logical clusters of scenes that will be shot together. Those strips are placed in a frame—called a strip board—*in the order they will be shot*. Remember, we don't start on page one of the script and shoot the movie in sequence; we break it down into scenes and then group the scenes and shoot them in a logical order from the standpoint of *cost efficiency*. The scheduling is dependent on numerous variables, such as season, whether the scenes are interior or exterior, actor availability, grouping scenes to reduce the cost of the cast, location availability and night shooting, among other things. So on day one of principal photography, we might shoot scenes seventy-one and thirty-two, and on day forty-three scenes one and one fifty-two. (Think what this means from a broad management perspective. Everything has to match perfectly in scenes that are shot weeks, even months, apart—sets, haircuts, tone of voice, screen direction, wardrobe, makeup, props, lighting, emotional tone, color palette . . .) I initially use the strips to schedule the film, and then, once we are shooting, I use the strip board to track our progress and make adjustments. For example, if we had scheduled to shoot an exterior on a particular day but rain is forecast and we move to an interior location, I adjust the strips accordingly. The board becomes the Bible or blueprint for the film's actual production process and assures us that nothing will be forgotten.

That fractional scheduling and extreme task segmentation carries through to every single part of the shooting day, as well. Every scene in a film—not just the stunts—is choreographed in a process called *blocking*, where the movements of each actor are laid out before we shoot. We decide where they will stand and move and then tape the floor so the actors know what marks to hit (where to walk, stand, move, and sit, and in what order). This process not only breaks the work down for each actor into small, clearly defined steps, but doing so, in turn, also breaks the work down for every other department, as well. Once we know where an actor will stand, sit, or move, we then know where to put the camera, lay dolly track, how and where to hang lights, what lens to use, and so on. This all becomes apparent as we parse the scene into choreographed steps during blocking.

The way this manifests is that instead of thinking about a hundred-page script to shoot, each day, on average, we focus on only two and a half pages. Those two and a half pages are comprised of scenes that are then broken down into a number of individual camera set ups, or shots. Director John McTiernan, "McT," (*Predator, Die Hard, The Hunt for Red October*) told me when we were working together on *Rollerball* that to him, "directing is a form of engineering." McT sometimes broke the shots down even further *by calculating the number of frames he needed*—he was thinking ahead to the editing room—saying perhaps, "I need twelve frames," which is a half second on-screen.[‡‡] One day we spent nearly five hours preparing and shooting what would end up being eight frames of a stuntman flying through the air after a motorcycle spill. We had parsed the action down to literally *one-third of a second of screen time*. Reduced like this, the work becomes clear, concise, and most important, *executable*. In the process of doing this extreme dissection, we transpose the daunting to the doable. And perhaps of more importance, it is

---

[‡‡] Dialogue is recorded at twenty-four frames per second, which is called synchronized sound speed. If a shot is done in slow motion, it may be shot at sixty frames per second, whereas high speed might be ten frames per second.

through that process of minute task dissection that bilateral trust develops between all the team members involved.

Here's why: *as each incremental step is laid out, every team member gains confidence that his or her incremental piece of the task is executable in a safe and productive manner.*

What this means is that the process of filmmaking starts with the whole project (overwhelming), and then we reduce it down to smaller sequenced and choreographed steps, which are in turn broken down into even tinier steps, which are then meticulously reduced to their component parts until we have a string of single tasks that everyone perceives as individually executable. In so doing, we're taking what Jim Collins and Jerry Porras call a *Big Hairy Audacious Goal* (BHAG)[§§]—in our case, making a feature film—and turning it into something incrementally executable. This type of extreme scheduling and task segmentation not only makes difficult tasks achievable, the incremental nature of the decision-making process and the planning and execution of those steps also builds confidence and trust—because it forces us to map out and communicate about even the smallest of details.

Now imagine that you just read the stunt sequence in the script for *F/X* for the first time. If you are the stuntman or one of the other professionals involved in filming that scene, you would know *exactly* how *parsed* and *dissected* and *tightly managed* the execution of that scene will be. And that will allow you to trust in the process whether you are the stuntman being lit on fire or the

---

[§§] Originally coined by Collins and Porras in their book *Built to Last: Successful Habits of Visionary Companies* in reference to vision statements and later used as a term to refer to large, amorphous business tasks that could benefit from segmentation.

person running the set who is responsible for that man's safety. There is another added, ancillary benefit, as well. Because this type of incremental task execution allows for what are known as "small wins"—that is, easily identifiable moments of progress—it also sets up something else that is very positive.

In 2011, researchers reported that incremental progress fuels feelings of well-being in workers and that those feelings of well-being fuel *further progress the following workday*. In other words, incremental, small successes or "wins" build the tensile strength of your team in a unique way. Teresa Amabile and Steven J. Kramer call it the "progress principle," and when they studied roughly 12,000 diary entries of 238 individuals at work, they recognized that even "minor progress evoked outsized positive reactions" that in turn created what they called a "progress loop" because they determined that those good feelings that arose from small achievements—wins—were drivers of *more achievement*. That translates to this: "small wins" not only fuel innovation and creativity in businesses employing agile development tactics, but when structured into *any* business, they are likely to be drivers of *motivation to work hard*, as well.***

The system of minute task segmentation and incremental work built around that *small-wins strategy* has been employed in day-to-day film production long before it became popular in tech innovation or Silicon Valley. We schedule a reasonable day's work with benchmark deadlines—we start the day with a call sheet that lists what scenes we are doing. That call sheet generates a specific

---

*** Small wins are used in tech industries for incremental product refinements and also in decision-making to mitigate risk.

shot list. Then we break those shots down into component parts for everyone involved. *And that sets the stage for small wins throughout the day—we get the first shot, the second shot, and so forth, creating an ongoing string of incremental accomplishments.*

When an amorphous project like making a feature film is broken down into fractional tasks, we are not only making a viable work schedule; we are also fueling productivity by building employee-manager trust. In addition, setting up what is an ongoing string of small wins also increases productivity in the workforce because it is a catalyst for motivation. *We all feel better when we can see and document progress, even if that progress is miniscule and incremental.* When this is embedded into the code of how we function, it works to establish needed trust between those executing a task and those managing it, thereby increasing the chances of success.

Insight:

A high level of trust between *those managing* and *those being managed* is imperative for the most successful outcomes.

Action Steps:
To build that trust:
Make sure you are the *emergent* as well as *assigned* leader.
Keep open communication.
Consider extreme task segmentation.
Create opportunities for small wins and progress loops.

Result:

Greater chance of successful task completion.

Higher confidence and cohesion.

Greater workplace safety and reduced stress.

REPLICATE THE "OSCAR EFFECT"

Improve Performance and Quality of Output by Cultivating a Self-Motivated Workforce

Case Study:

The film *Sabrina*. Paramount Pictures. Directed by Sydney Pollack; starring Harrison Ford, Julia Ormond, and Greg Kinnear.

LATE ONE NIGHT, as I stepped out of a restaurant in Providence, Rhode Island, a simple observation led to a critical insight about employee engagement and self-directed motivation. This area of the city is primarily comprised of tall office buildings clustered around a green, and at that hour of the night, it was a ghost town. As I walked back to my hotel, I noticed that all the buildings around me were completely dark, except for one.

Ours.

Standing in front of the only building with lights on, I counted up from the lobby, and sure enough, it was our fourth-floor production offices that were lit up. Counting over from my office, I deduced that it was the wardrobe designer and her assistant who were working so late. I knew that they worked on a flat, weekly salary, so they weren't being paid overtime, and I also knew that no one had told them to stay late—they were doing so of their own volition. This type of diligence and drive is not atypical in filmmaking—it's actually commonplace.

As a frontline manager of large work crews, standing on that sidewalk at 10:00 P.M. and knowing that employees with a strong work ethic are critical to the success of every business, the question I asked myself wasn't, *Why is the wardrobe department working late?* It was, *Why is this behavior so normal in the film industry?* Especially in light of the fact that employee *disengagement* and *lack of motivation* is extremely prevalent—and costly—on both a domestic and a global basis. As a manager, I also knew that the direct dollar impact of high levels of employee disengagement is only the tip of the iceberg—*unmotivated, disengaged employees also decrease workplace cohesion and fluidity of work flow, lower the quality of the goods produced or services rendered, and cripple innovation.*

If we couple that high employee disengagement and lack of self-directed motivation with *inefficiencies*, the outcomes get worse. Remember that assembly line worker at Harley Davidson who calculated that it took each worker an extra 1.2 seconds to snap in a particular motorcycle part because of a fault in its design that resulted in an annual production deficit of 2,200 machines and millions of dollars in lost revenue for the company? You want an employee who figures something like that out to be highly motivated to point that problem out to management. If employees are not engaged and motivated, they likely won't, and when you consider the myriad seemingly miniscule "faulty parts," and 1.2-second inefficiencies that occur in every business, it's easy to see the multiplier effect poor motivation can have and just how Goliath-like a management problem disengaged, unmotivated employees can be.

These codependent, self-perpetuating issues of poor motivation and inefficiency often go unaddressed—or are superficially addressed—by business leaders and managers because all those micro measures of efficiency and the intangibles of motivation are hard to quantify on an individual basis. And to be honest, it's also because it seems that even if we do identify and measure them, there's no clear way for us to improve these metrics anyway. Let's face it: when we try to increase motivation—even with raises and bonuses—many of our efforts fail.

But that night in Providence when our wardrobe designer and her assistant were capping off a long workday with a long work night with no external mandate to do so, I deduced that there had to be specific, unique factors in the film industry that fostered this type of extreme diligence and self-motivation. And as I was standing there thinking about it, a long list of examples of this highly desirable, tensile-strength-building, productivity-escalating behavior from other film projects flashed through my mind—and not just examples of hard work and self-imposed long hours—but also above-and-beyond-the-call-of-duty examples of exceptional innovation and creative effort, as well.

Over the years, I had witnessed numerous occasions when a crew had gone the extra mile to get a shot before the sun came up or jury-rigged a creative solution at 2:00 A.M. with the union clock running and the earth spinning toward sunup, and in all those examples it would have been a whole lot easier to *not* speak up or simply say, "*No, it can't be done*," or "*We don't have enough time.*" I recall being at the end of a long night of shooting in a high school football stadium in Beaufort, South Carolina, on *The Prince of Tides* when Barbra Streisand (the director) asked about the possibility of adding an intricate and challenging shot before we wrapped. She wanted a moving camera to creep along very slowly and discover Nick Nolte sitting alone in the dark on the stadium steps. This presented a technical and logistical challenge because of the steep slope of the steps and the enormous weight of the camera and dolly. Stephen Goldblatt (the director of photography) and I were discussing how difficult this would be to pull off when Bobby Ward, one of the truly great key grips, volunteered that he could run twelve feet of dolly track at an oblique angle down the stadium tiers and then cantilever the dolly* by hanging counterweights over the side of the bleachers to balance the five hundred–pound load, and he convinced us that it was doable. And it was—we got the shot.

I remember a propman on the Woody Allen film *A Midsummer Night's Sex Comedy* stepping into thigh-deep water in a stream in his street clothes to save time; no waders, no boots, no thought of saying, "Can you wait ten minutes while I grab my gear?" I recall a production designer in Memphis, Tennessee, on the film *Nothing But the Truth* in tears because she was worried that she might not have the set she was designing and building of an exact replica of the interior of the United States Supreme Court ready in time. We're talking the Supreme Court here—gigantic marble columns, the wooden desk where the judges sit, the burgundy

---

* A wheeled cart on which a camera is mounted.

drapes . . . It took more than four years to build the original—she had two weeks to replicate it, and the thought that she might need an extra day left her in tears.

I also remember working on *Sabrina* when we were scheduled to film a picnic scene with Harrison Ford and Julia Ormond at night on a beach on Martha's Vineyard and the production designer, Brian Morris, volunteered to director Sydney Pollack that he could duplicate the beach on the stage back in New York. Since, creatively, Sydney decided that he didn't need any really wide shots, the scene was containable and buildable. By filming it on a soundstage back in New York, rather than on an actual beach on Martha's Vineyard at night as we had originally scheduled and planned, we could bring the actors in at 7:00 in the morning and shoot what we call *day for night*. This meant we wouldn't be doing close-ups at three in the morning when the actors wouldn't look their best. Building the beach set on a soundstage also meant that we would have total control of the environment—no wind blowing Julia Ormond's hair across her face, no pounding waves presenting a challenge for the sound department. No threat of rain or the need for extra time spent lighting a night exterior. On top of that, the set could be designed exactly how Sydney wanted it to look—from the shape and size of the sand dunes to the distance to the water and the quality of the night sky. In addition, shot options increased, and the crew would be rolling equipment across a stage, not humping it down to the water's edge in the dark. Plus, if we shot the scene back in New York, we'd save $30,000 a day on the hundred-plus cast and crew we now had in hotels and were paying per diem to. So this option would save a great deal of money on the business end, and at the same time it would give the director creative freedom and control.

The thing of it was, the production designer on *Sabrina* didn't *have to suggest this*. In fact, it created much more work for him and his department, and he, of course, had no vested interest in saving the company money on hotels and per diem. In fact, he's exactly the type of motivated, engaged employee that you want on your team because he's taking initiative and going above and beyond what's expected; he's just like the employee at Harley David- son working on the line and observing a way for the company to save money—and in our case simultaneously improving creative output—and reporting it to management.

So by the time I got to my hotel room in Providence that night, I was asking myself, *Who cries at work instead of explaining that she might need an extra day or two to meet a tight deadline? Who wades into the water in his street clothes to save the company a few minutes? Who goes out of his way to suggest a change in the schedule that means more work for him but a better outcome for the project?* Especially since most managers in the larger business environment are banging their heads against walls trying to figure out how to motivate employees just to do what's expected.

I was able to isolate *four very specific factors* that are unique to filmmaking that help explain this high level of individual em- ployee engagement and what is an almost universal industry- and crew-wide, high level of self-directed motivation to not just do a *good, solid professional job* but to go above and beyond that and *excel*.

- First, filmmakers work in a small, closed industry based on a gig economy. That means we are dependent on the quality of our work and the commercial and artistic success of our current project in order to get future jobs. And because we work freelance and our projects cycle so quickly, getting a new job is something we all need to do several times a year. That requires reputation building and positive peer recommendations—a structure that is a huge factor in motivating a very high level of effort.

- Second, the behavioral science behind intrinsic motivation predicts that when employees are offered new challenges and novel experiences that can lead to growth and self-development, it increases motivation even more than concrete rewards like salary increases. Each film project offers a staggering array of unique challenges, novelty of experience, and the opportunity for growth.

- Third, it's a lot easier to slack and not care about the quality of your work if the quality of what you do isn't directly attributed to you *personally* or if it isn't really seen by anyone outside of your own company. In the film business, department heads and key personnel know that their work will be subject to very *public scrutiny*. After all, our work appears in theaters and on television *with our names on it*; it doesn't get much more public than that.

- And fourth, the Oscars, Golden Globes, and other industry awards offer *very public, industry-endorsed recognition for excellence*. Those award nominations and wins *leverage and propel careers* for the people who get them—they translate into more job offers and higher-profile projects in the future. That leads to higher pay, more creative opportunity and prestige, and the chance for even *more* recognition.

What I understood by the time I fell asleep that night was that the frequent need to get hired on new jobs, the opportunity for unique challenges, and the public display of work coupled with a system of globally televised awards works in concert to create and perpetuate employee motivation for high achievement. After standing on that sidewalk that night looking up at those lit windows shining brightly in a business world crippled by too many dark windows, I started thinking about those four elements as the "Oscar Effect" because I understood that, taken together, they are a management superfecta for this reason: *because of them, I am able to work under the assumption that most of the crew will kill themselves to excel at their jobs.*

And while that makes my job as a manager much, much easier, I also recognized that managers in *any* business can replicate these elements to self-motivate *their* employees, as well.

MANY MANAGERS AT companies where employees work on commission or have stock options, the potential to receive lucrative bonuses, or competitive promotions often have similarly self-motivated employees. But the reality is that many, if not most, managers face the *exact opposite scenario*—they are managing a workforce that is *not* self-motivated (internally or externally) to perform at the highest level. In fact, most managers find—and the data backs this up—that most employees are highly *unmotivated* to perform. Which means that you as a manager have to assess which of these two categories your workforce falls into—and the reason for this is twofold and straightforward.

First, these two groups need to be *managed differently*.

And second, if your employees *aren't* in the highly engaged and self-motivated group, there are simple changes in your management strategy that can completely turn that around.

In other words, no matter what your business, you can create your own version of the Oscar Effect.

To do this involves, again, *inverting control*.

Which means that you need to stop thinking about the lack of employee motivation as a problem *employees need to remedy* and start thinking of it as an issue for *you as a manager to fix*.

That single change in management perspective instantly alters everything for this reason:

Once you take ownership of a problem, you are taking the first step toward correcting it.

With that single change in your manager-employee worldview, you, as a manager, are no longer a victim of employee disengagement; you are in a position to disarm it. As a manager who is solely focused on building the tensile strength of your team by writing managerial code that will invert control and automate positive behavior, what could be better than taking control of what is a global issue of employee disengagement and lack of motivation and turning it around at your company or on your team?

By rethinking the internal dynamics of your managerial strategy, you can fundamentally change the work ethic of your staff—and this can be achieved by changing some *small things* that lie in that management superfecta.

First, replicate some elements of the gig economy by *creating a feeling of ownership of, and accountability for, the quality of what you produce in the entire workforce.*[†]

Second, *embed novel experiences and growth opportunities for all employees.*

Third, *structure a systemic way to emphasize pride in work.*

And fourth, *provide some degree of public- or industry-level scrutiny*—not on the scale of the Oscars, of course, but just enough to create an incremental shift in productivity and quality of output.

BEFORE I EXPLAIN the specifics of how you might actually do this, it's worth considering the compounding benefits of doing so. For starters, in the film business this high level of internal drive and motivation may begin with department heads, but it then has a *trickle-down* and a *trickle-across* effect. Department heads in each specialized unionized area of expertise—production, cinematography, sound, property, set design, makeup and hair, wardrobe, transportation, grip and electric—get hired to do a film, and those department heads in turn hire the staff for their respective departments. In an industry structured where higher-ups depend on reputation and body of work to get jobs several times a year, and where lower-echelon employees depend on *those* higher-ups to secure *their* jobs, it increases the likelihood that the work of each and every employee in every department will be of the absolute highest quality.

[†] The value of doing this was well documented by the brilliant work of W. Edwards Deming in Japan in the 1960s.

On a film project, the third set dresser will never get an Oscar, but if the department head does—because he or she does the hiring—then that third set dresser is motivated to do a great job so he or she will be hired for bigger and better projects secured by the Oscar-winning department head in the future. Those bigger and better projects also translate to higher pay, the opportunity for faster career advancement, and the chance to work with higher-tier people, which leads to greater creative opportunities and more high-level contacts for networking future jobs. If your choice as a filmmaker is between two projects—say, working on a $3 million independent film shot in the Bronx at night with a first-time director, an unknown cast, and second-tier crew—or working on a $60 million studio picture like *Sabrina* that will be shot in New York City, Paris, and Martha's Vineyard with Oscar-winning producer Scott Rudin,[‡] Oscar-winning director Sydney Pollack,[§] the world-class cinematographer Giuseppe Rotunno,[**] the legendary Oscar-winning wardrobe designer Ann Roth,[††] and actors like Harrison Ford and Julia Ormond, it's usually not too hard to decide which project to pick.

Bringing this concept back to the Hollywood principle, we are looking for ways to rewrite our managerial code with simple changes in how we operate and by altering the instructions that we give, and we want the positive effects of *that* code and *those*

[‡] *No Country for Old Men, The Girl with the Dragon Tattoo, Captain Phillips, The Social Network.*

[§] *Out of Africa, Three Days of the Condor, The Interpreter, The Yakuza, The Way We Were.*

[**] Known for his work with Federico Fellini; *Roma, Amarcord, Satyricon,* and nominated for an Oscar for *All That Jazz.*

[††] *The English Patient, The Hours, The Talented Mr. Ripley, The Bird Cage.*

instructions *to invoke automatically* whenever possible, so we have to *do less as we achieve more.* So here's the best part:

Once some employees are motivated, others become so, too, and not just vertically within departments but horizontally across departments, as well.

That means that for a manager consciously making these changes, it has a contagious, ripple effect. Ron Friedman calls this *motivational synchronicity. We unconsciously pick up on the behavior of those around us and mimic it.* That means if some employees are working hard, other employees will see that and act in the same manner, too.

If you think that drive and motivation aren't something you can change as a manager or that motivation isn't structure driven or "codeable" in your industry or business, consider the following example of the Oscar Effect at work from outside the film business.

"A $1.25 FEE will be added to every meal to allow us to offer full benefits to our employees."

With this single sentence, Jennifer Piallat, the owner of Zazie in San Francisco, was able to create her own Oscar Effect by making one small change that allowed her to alter the motivation of her employees, increase her profit (by 300 percent), lower her stress as a manager, and improve the quality of the food and service in her restaurant. With that $1.25, Piallat was able to provide higher pay, a bonus program, and full benefits—including health and dental care, maternity and paternity leave, and matching 401(k)s—along with stable work schedules to her full restaurant staff. On top of all of that, she was able to disrupt long-standing managerial problems of high turnover and disengaged, unmotivated employees in an industry rife with them.[‡‡]

In other words, she implemented a simple change that increased the tensile strength of her organization and improved her bottom line, and she did so in a manner that, once this small change was initiated, became *automated*—the positive outcomes continued with little additional effort on her part.

In fact, what she did was simple and transformational, and she managed to accomplish it in an industry plagued with both high employee turnover *and* poor motivation.

Every manager knows why this matters; an employee with one foot out the door who knows that he or she will have no trouble getting another similar, low-paying, relatively thankless job somewhere else is not highly motivated to show up on time and do a great job. And that *lack of employee motivation* is actually built into the structural underpinnings of the restaurant industry just as *high motivation and engagement* is built into the structure of the film industry.

Why was Piallat's solution so inspired? And why did she decide to involve patrons in this financial decision? After all, she could have just increased the price of a meal by $1.25 and provided her employees with full benefits without saying anything to diners—or not provided benefits at all and pocketed the additional profit herself.

[‡‡] According to the Bureau of Labor Statistics, turnover in the restaurant business was 66.3 percent in 2014.

But she likely understood two things:

By posting it on the menu, she provided public validation, which is an important factor in that increase in employee motivation.

Her profit would rise more by increasing employee motivation and engagement than by a direct-to-her-pocket menu price increase.

Piallat was able to create a real sense of ownership in what those employees were producing; she gave them a common goal, which functioned to alter the motivation and accountability of her staff. She structured a systematic way to provide job stability and reduce turnover and emphasize new challenges and pride in work. She provided some degree of public scrutiny and changed how what she was selling was perceived by the marketplace. What she saw after this change was implemented was that her profit increased by more than the $1.25 per meal when she used the $1.25 to provide stabilizing benefits to her employees. In effect, with one small change, she was able to alter the focus of her entire staff from thinking about how *I* can succeed *for me* to how can *we* succeed as a team *for us*, and from what can *I* slough off to someone else to what I *have to do* as a member of a team for the collective good of the business. And she did it in a way that led to accountability and pride in work.

And of course Jen Piallat isn't the only manger doing this. Many restaurant managers are moving in this direction, and there are numerous examples from other industries of companies achieving a high level of motivation by tweaking their policies, as well. Andrew M. Thompson, the CEO of Proteus, a biomedical company based in Redwood City, California, has a system of peer-nominated excellence where employees are given gold coins for recognition. Sales companies often have a salesman ring a bell when a sale is made. Maynard Webb, Yahoo's chairman, asks his team leaders, "You have seven people working for you. How many of those would you rehire if all the positions were open again?" Then consider how the ride-sharing service Uber employs public scrutiny via service ratings to motivate employees in an industry that has traditionally been an environment where employees could get away with poor performance without any broad repercussions. Uber was able to motivate good behavior from drivers simply by instituting a rating system visible to Uber management and potential passengers. In so doing, they inverted control—took it from the drivers who usually have it in the taxi industry and gave it to passengers and management. Since Uber drivers lose their right to work for the company if their ratings fall too low on a 1–5 scale (at 4.6, they are at risk for losing the right to drive), they kill themselves to be on time, polite, open doors, drive safely, stay off the phone, have a clean car, offer passengers water, and so on. And this is a self-correcting algorithm, not just a simple 1–5 rating scale.

Here's why.

As with all averages, an extreme early rating is more heavily weighted than an extreme later rating. A driver who has hundreds of pickups and a high rating won't drop much due to a single poor score—but a new driver with a single poor rating will likely be fired immediately (remember, a rating below a 4.6 puts you at risk for being fired). This weeds out the bad drivers almost as soon as they are hired. And, interestingly, the drivers get to rate the passengers as well, which weeds out poor passengers, too—passengers who are rude, late, drunk, and so on. In the Uber model, a poorly rated passenger likely won't get picked up by a driver who gets the pickup ping, so this rating feature functions as a self-correcting, self-regulating system that removes both bad drivers *and* bad passengers from the system—again with very little monitoring on the part of management.

Compare this to traditional taxicab companies that have little or no control over driver performance or passenger behavior—usually the worst that would happen to a driver for poor performance would be that he or she wouldn't get a tip—and rude passengers are completely anonymous, as well. Uber, on the other hand, has quite a bit of control over driver performance and passenger behavior, and that control is built into the system. On top of that, they've gamed it—meaning that many Uber drivers become obsessed with and take great pride in their ratings. And the best part is that Uber management doesn't have to do anything to get high performance from its drivers—or good behavior from their passengers—it's automated. HomeAdvisor, Angie's List, and others have done a similar thing by motivating a high level of performance from contractors by allowing potential customers to see previous customers' ratings. What I am purporting isn't micromanaging; it's the exact opposite. It's the Hollywood principle and inversion of control—*Don't call us, we'll call you*. It's the hands-free management that results *when the system is structured to give you as a manager what you want, automatically.*

Now consider the hands-free, automated, *motivational*

synchronicity multiplier effect of this. Think about Uber drivers competing with other drivers for the highest ratings. Or a new hire at Zazie who witnesses a hardworking busboy who, because of the appeal of profit sharing, high pay, health insurance, a 401(k) with matching funds, and a stable work schedule in an industry not known for that, isn't out back having a cigarette— he's bending over backward to keep his job and taking pride and ownership of the creative output of the entire team, making sure that all the seats and tables are immaculate. He doesn't wait for a manager to tell him to go clear a table or refill water glasses; he's got eyes and hands on it even *before* the manager does. With every employee having skin in the game, no one will be turning a blind eye to a fellow employee who is slacking off, either. Any new employee witnessing this work ethic picks up a message from that behavior, and *that* benefits the company.

Consider the flip side of motivational synchronicity. If you have poorly motivated employees with a poor work ethic, that *lack of motivation* spreads, too. Which means that changing the management underpinnings in a way that alters the motivation of some members of your workforce changes outcomes because it has the power to *proliferate throughout the team* as it provides positive behavior models and allows managers to completely invert the high level of employee disengagement that plagues most businesses.

An interesting dynamic of this for me as the manager of these highly motivated department heads is that extreme motivation to perform can create, right alongside all that hard work and collaboration, interdepartmental *competition for resources*—which in our case is everyone clamoring for more time and money so they can do *an even better job.* Since we have a single common goal—making a great film—and highly segmented jobs, there is no *direct competition* between departments. However, there is so much motivation to excel that there is often competition *between* departments for resources because everyone is trying so hard to deliver and be recognized for excellence. Actors want more takes, more coverage, and the best lines. Cinematographers want more time to light and set up elaborate and innovative shots. Production designers want bigger budgets and more time to create sets. Arrangers want the latitude to compose and perform more original music. Wardrobe designers want more resources to showcase their work . . .

If you think about it, as a manager of a cross-functional team—in a broader business environment where nearly 75 percent of those teams are dysfunctional—these are enviable problems to have.

INSIGHT:

Creating a highly self-motivated workforce improves outcomes across all success metrics.

Action Steps:
Replicate the Oscar Effect:
> Create a feeling of ownership of, and accountability for, the quality of what you produce in your entire workforce.
> Embed novel experiences and growth opportunities for all employees.

Structure a systemic way to emphasize pride in work.
Provide some degree of public- or industry-level scrutiny.

Result:
Automated motivational synchronicity.
Less oversight needed.
Better innovation.
Highest possible productivity and increased profit.

ACCOMMODATE EMPLOYEES

─────────────✦─────────────

CASE STUDY:
The film *Uptown Girls*. MGM. Directed by Boaz Yakin; starring
Brittany Murphy, Dakota Fanning, and Heather Locklear.

───

ADOPTING AND THEN modifying the four component elements
of the Oscar Effect in an industry- or company-specific way—*the
frequent need we have to get new jobs,* the unique challenges and
opportunities for growth, the ownership and "public" display of work,
and a system of high-visibility workplace awards*—is only the first
step in cultivating the highest possible level of workplace engagement and employee motivation. The next step is to identify *any
specific benefits and accommodations* (over and above any preexisting
union or regulatory mandates in your industry or at your com-

---

* Think about the fact that the owner of Zazie reverse engineered the issue of
job insecurity to motivate employees who *didn't* want to move from job to
job—there are numerous ways to adapt this concept.

pany) that can be leveraged to increase motivation to an even higher degree. The trick is for managers to look at all the benefits and accommodations available to them and question which are the *true motivators* and which of them may *sound good on paper* but *don't actually work*. Even more important is to identify any employee benefits and personal accommodations that are available to you, or that you are already providing with good intentions, that may actually *function to disengage the workforce*.

I frequently have to make *complicated* and *extreme* accommodations for individual employees—say, scheduling around other projects and commitments, arranging for dialogue coaches, personal makeup artists, masseuses, technical advisors, multiple motor homes, and personal trainers or dramatically increasing a departmental budget—and as I'm making these accommodations, I've often reflected on how managers in far more conventional businesses often resist or resent making even *small* accommodations for their employees and how often that fact interferes with those employees doing their jobs. (Think of requests for flex hours, telecommuting, or reimbursement for job-related expenses that are not covered but probably should be.)

When thinking about accommodations and benefits as a means to elevate employee motivation to excel, it helps to look at them as falling into three natural divisions. First, there are the accommodations that we have no choice in; we make these accommodations or give these benefits to meet laws, policy, and regulations. These mandates may be expensive or annoying, but they add structure and become part of what I call the "hard corners"—that is, *those concrete elements that anchor our decisions*. I know, for example, that in my industry, union rules dictate *exactly* when I have to break for lunch and *exactly* what the penalty will be if I don't, and that helps me frame decisions about whether to buy a meal penalty (pay a higher hourly crew rate to keep shooting) or break for lunch.

Second, there are the accommodations we make and benefits we offer that are *optional* but that we feel we *have to offer in order to be competitive and attract and retain top-tier talent and get a high level of performance from employees.* These vary by industry and are fairly obvious, as well—things like competitive salaries, health insurance, paid vacation, or perhaps summer hours.

Third, there are the accommodations we make and the benefits we offer that are *completely discretionary* but that help us attract and retain the highest tier of talent and are instrumental in motivating employees to perform at the highest levels. These may include more and better versions of the benefits mentioned above, as well as more intangible things that fall under the umbrella of individual needs and company culture.

From a practical standpoint, we have to accept the first category of accommodations and benefits as *irrefutable mandates.* Then an effective way to make improvements in the two "optional" tiers is to determine *which* accommodations and benefits we *should* be offering by assessing *which of them deliver and which don't.*

In a move parallel to that of Jennifer Piallat, the owner of Zazie, recently Bobby Fry, the founder of restaurant Bar Marco in Pittsburgh, decided to end tipping and to give employees a set base salary of $35,000 (plus bonuses based on profit, which are expected to bring salaries to between $48,000 and $51,000), health benefits, five hundred shares of company stock, and paid vacations. Just one month after the policy change, Fry reported that his profit *tripled* on a revenue increase of 26 percent. He attributes the high rise in profit relative to his revenue increase to the cumulative impact of a retooled menu and lower overhead that resulted from greater employee diligence that *he* instigated by offering compelling benefits. Fry saw his water, linen, and liquor bills drop and his profit escalate. By making these changes in pay structure and benefits, Fry instituted *ownership of outcome* and a *common unified goal* through *shared profit*. Fry did so by implementing *small changes that had a big impact* in a remarkably instantaneous, win-win, and sustainable way.

But now consider that a number of restaurants across the country have tried at least parts of this model with a different outcome. The Quilted Giraffe in New York instituted a service charge in place of tipping back in the 1980s, and the policy failed. Brett Cooper and the Daniel Patterson Group tried no tipping at Aster in the Mission District of San Francisco when it opened in 2015 and quickly decided it wasn't going to work. So while these were iterations of the same theme successfully used by Piallat and Fry, the question is, *why did it work in some cases and not in others?*

And the answer to this is never easy, but what it illustrates is this: in order to increase employee motivation, we not only have to get the *individual benefits* right but we also have to make sure to package them in the right *combinations*, as well. And that is going to be tricky for all of us.

The key is finding out what works and what doesn't and *in what combinations* at our particular company, and to do that mandates taking a close look at *why we accommodate employees in the first place.*

CASE IN POINT: Moo.

On the film *Uptown Girls*, the script called for a small pet pig named Moo. That meant we actually had to "hire" a pig, which in turn meant that I would have to *manage a pig*—and *that* would prove to be complicated and problematic from the onset.

For starters, in the pig world, "small and cute" is a transient state. A farm pig rapidly grows to weigh a thousand pounds—or more—and, despite what most people think, even a pig from a miniature breed will quickly reach 120–150 pounds. The translation of this was that our target employee was a miniature potbellied pig between six and eight weeks of age.

When I was scheduling the film and we were hiring the cast (including Moo), it was two and a half months *before* we were to commence principal photography. That meant that any cute little pigs (piglets six to eight weeks old at the time) that the breeders brought us to look at would grow to be over one hundred pounds by the time we needed them for filming. After meeting with pig breeders and animal trainers, we decided that our best option was to contract to breed two pigs (in case the piglet got sick or injured or was impossibly uncooperative) that would be the right size during the window of time that we had scheduled to shoot the scenes—an original Moo and a backup Moo.

Under normal circumstances, scheduling a film project is a meticulous process that takes into account more variables than you can imagine—from actor and location availability to weather and seasons to streamlining company moves to incorporating myriad budgetary considerations like the cost savings when consolidating actors' schedules.[†] In this particular case, I also had to accommodate

---

[†] If I can consolidate an individual actor's work into five weeks, we pay him or her for five weeks—not, say, seven or eight weeks or "run of the picture." That can potentially—depending on who the actors are and how many actors you can do this for—save hundreds of thousands of dollars.

for pig gestation (110–115 days), the time needed for pig training, and the fact that one of our employees was going to "age out" by growing at a rapid rate—possibly doubling in size in just a few weeks. All these immovable pieces would dictate when Moo should be born and when we could shoot the piglet scenes—and *that* in turn affected the scheduling of the entire film.

Further complicating the scheduling process was that Moo's scenes would have to be shot close together (blocked) to accommodate her fast rate of growth, and I had to consider the time needed prior to shooting for Moo and backup Moo to be trained to perform some very specific tasks by responding to a clicker and food treats. It also meant that we had to keep a pig trainer and handler on the payroll. All of this would take time, money, and planning upfront and a boatload of patience when we were actually shooting. And due to Moo's projected growth trajectory, I had to give careful thought to the fact that once we committed to the schedule, we would have virtually no flexibility.

Going into the shoot, I also understood that working with a pig meant that we would be dealing with *a high degree of unpredictability across the board*. Even if the pig's performance was perfect, there were so many other non-pig-related variables that could go wrong in these scenes, as well. *The camera operator overpans, the first assistant cameraman misses focus, the dolly grip's timing is off, the soundman dips the boom into frame, an actress blows a line . . .* To get a printable take, *everyone* in front of *and* behind the camera had to do his or her job perfectly—not just the pig.

Then there was the fact that the script called for giving Moo a bubble bath.

To streamline and facilitate the bubble bath scene, we built the bathroom set on a soundstage in order to easily accommodate our equipment and personnel (it's hard to squeeze a film crew and equipment into a typical residential bathroom) and we ran multiple cameras to allow us to get the coverage we needed in a single take. On the day of shooting, we went with a skeleton crew on set since the pigs were skittish around large numbers of people. Despite these efforts, when we went to actually shoot the scene, as well trained as she was, Moo decided that (at least on that day) she didn't like the water—or the bubbles. On top of that, when she was placed in the tub and her hooves slipped on the porcelain, it caused her to out-and-out panic. That in turn led to excessive squealing and frantic behavior and raised potentially serious concerns about the comfort and stress level of Moo from the ASPCA rep we were required to have on set.

In response, we removed Moo from the water, sent her to be calmed down by the trainer, and began a series of modifications—including lining the tub with thick rubber mats. But even with all the accommodations, during the bubble bath, Moo continued to squeal and splash far more than we wanted from a creative standpoint, and that meant additional takes and numerous wardrobe changes for the two actresses—Dakota Fanning and Brittany Murphy—who were bathing her. That slowed us down and meant we were burning through the shooting day—and cash—like a hog goes through feed.

Now consider for a moment that all the accommodations I just described were being made for *a single employee*—and we had *thousands of employees* on this project. For example, one of the leading actresses, Dakota Fanning, was only nine years old, and because she was so young, she needed her own set of specific accommodations, as well.[‡]

What is interesting about this particular story is how far we went to hire, train, and accommodate an *individual employee*—Moo. We actually *bred the employee* (along with a spare), spent a hefty sum to build an animatronic backup, adjusted our schedule around her needs, carefully trained her, and made extensive physical workplace accommodations.

Why?

Because we needed her.

And we needed Moo to be in a very specific physical and psychological state in order for her to be able to do her job well. In this case, that involved looking small and cute and stealing the hearts of film viewers while performing her "acting" tasks. In order to do *that*, she had to be a specific size, well trained, and *reasonably happy*.

Note that at no point were we accommodating Moo *to be nice*. Nor were we doing it to project a good corporate image, attract other employees to the company, or be politically correct—reasons that often drive employee benefits and accommodations. Rather, we were making all these accommodations for Moo because they were necessary in order for her to do a job *for us*.

In fact, everything we did, every expense, and every accommodation we made was *self-serving*.

[‡] For example, child labor laws restricted her workday to eight hours *inclusive* of three hours of tutoring, one hour for lunch, travel to and from the set, and time needed for makeup, hair, and wardrobe—which left her with approximately three hours of actual shooting time per day. And of course, numerous additional accommodations are made for individual actors—especially if they are children.

And we don't just do this for animals. As noted, we make extreme accommodations for people all the time, too.

Once a manager understands that many accommodations serve the *employer* rather than the *employee*, it can alter our perspective and course of action regarding making accommodations for individual employees—whether those accommodations are corporate-wide like health insurance[§] or are based on specific individual employee needs (in our case, putting a rubber mat on the floor of a bathtub).

In the case of Moo, although the accommodations we needed to make to secure the results we wanted were complicated and well thought out, they presented themselves in a pretty obvious manner. But that's often far from typical with human employees. There is an abundance of social science research that confirms what most of us likely already suspect—that our brains don't always function in easy-to-understand, set patterns. And that means that finding the right employee benefits and accommodations to offer (and in what combinations) can feel downright impossible or at the very least be a frustrating and painfully time-consuming and expensive process.

WHEN YOU CONSIDER that the work of numerous behavioral researchers, including Harry F. Harlow and Edward Deci, reveals

---

[§] In October 2014, Walmart joined Home Depot and Target in canceling health insurance coverage for over thirty thousand part-time employees. This will save the company money—but also *negatively* impact the ability of those employees to do their jobs. Without health coverage, they will be out sick more, suffer the financial hardship of higher health care costs, and have less loyalty to the employer.

that immediate rewards—say, a raise or promotion (or a squirt of juice or a pellet of food for lab animals)—motivate in the short run but *don't motivate behavior over the long term*, we begin to see that finding and implementing the right employee accommodations and benefits is probably more complex than we might hope. Working in a lab with rhesus monkeys in 1949, Harlow discovered that *intrinsic motivation—the innate desire to solve novel problems—*works more consistently as a motivational force than an *immediate food treat*.

This is, on the one hand, *encouraging* (and why I included novel experiences and opportunity for growth as one of the factors in the Oscar Effect). It's good to know that there is an inborn natural curiosity that manifests as an internal drive to accomplish. On the other hand, it's *discouraging* since it suggests that a simple-to-execute, incentive-based reward structure is not likely to be the best way to motivate employees consistently over time. To make matters worse, in a continuation of Harlow's work, two decades later, Edward Deci found that immediate rewards can actually *decrease* motivation over the long term. Couple these daunting, counterintuitive insights with Maslow's progressive hierarchy of needs** and Richard M. Ryan and Edward L. Deci's self-determination theory (SDT)—which states that the desire for autonomy, competence, and relatedness drive motivation and behavior—then add Deming's work on drivers of motivation—including ownership of outcome—in the workplace, and what

---

** Abraham Maslow's hierarchy of motivation progresses from the need to satisfy basic needs to safety needs to social needs to self-esteem and finally self-actualization.

we see is that the mechanism behind motivating employees is often not direct and linear. Instead of following B. F. Skinner's simple model of operant conditioning—positive reinforcement leads to an increase in desired behavior—what we see is that workplace motivation is a rather nuanced amalgam of complex cognitive and behavioral interactions.

Let's say you are managing a tech company hoping to attract top-tier talent. You don't necessarily have the four key factors of the Oscar Effect at your disposal—you don't have public displays of work or industry awards, and your workers don't necessarily have jobs with novel challenges (at least not all of them) or have the requisite need to get a new job several times a year—in fact, you *want these employees to stay as long as possible*—maybe even for life. So as a manager, you do a few things to recognize accomplishments at work—maybe set up awards and recognition ceremonies—but let's face it, there are all sorts of available employee accommodations beyond those four that should be able to motivate employees to work hard. You feel that in your industry you need different, more compelling, even *bespoke motivators*.

So as a means to attract and keep top talent, you step outside the typical grab bag of HR benefits and pedestrian, run-of-the-mill accommodations, and you do something counterintuitive; you offer all employees *unlimited vacation time*. You make it corporate policy for employees to *take off as much time as they want*. And what happens? If your employees are anything like the employees at Kickstarter and Evernote, when you offer them unlimited vacation time—called discretionary time off (DTO) in Human Resource lingo—it makes headlines and wows those of us on the outside who are first blindsided with envy but then start thinking,

Wait, how will that work? And then, while most of us have visions of spending the whole summer at the beach while still collecting our paychecks, we find out that people at companies offering unlimited vacation time aren't at the beach at all; in fact, they take *less vacation time under this model than they did when they were restricted to two or three weeks each year.* Talk about an amalgam of complex cognitive and behavioral nuance and entanglements. Who would have predicted that?

As a manager, you're thinking, you just offered your employees endless days off, *so why aren't they taking advantage of it?* Then you find out, as the CEO of Evernote did, that this *no-one-will-go-on-vacation-problem* is even worse than you'd thought. *You notice that most of your employees with unlimited vacation days aren't even taking five consecutive days off in a year—so you sweeten the pot and throw in a stipend of $1,000 in cash to do so.* And *that* doesn't even work. You read that another company, FullContact, pays their employees a stipend of $7,500 if they take all their vacation days—that is, as long as they don't call in to the office or check e-mail. Then you read that RAND Corporation pays employees an extra 3–5% of their salary for vacation days taken. Next, you discover that Kickstarter decided to end their unlimited vacation day policy because employees felt guilty and took *less time* rather than *more time* when vacation days were declared "unlimited."

What *specifically* is stopping employees from taking advantage of days off, even when they are limited? Part of the explanation lies in fears over job security and employees angling for promotions and career advancement and concerns over work accumulation. Also, since some companies must pay employees for any vacation days they are entitled to but don't actually take, it means that some employees are tempted by a cash payout for unused vacation and sick days.††

But there is more to these decisions than *practicality*.

Part of the reason for the failure of what would seem on the surface to be an unbelievable perk—unlimited vacation time—is related to the psychological constraints of "choice architecture,"‡‡ and it's complicated—and clearly not fully understood. Sheena Iyengar, a professor at Columbia Business School, refers to this as "choice overload." Barry Schwartz, the Dorwin Cartwright professor of Social Theory and Social Action at Swarthmore College, calls it the "Tyranny of Choice."§§ In simple terms, it means that too many options can lead people to feel overwhelmed and therefore be indecisive.

And indeed, many suspect that the take-as-many-days-off-as-you-want model lands employees overwhelmed with choice and burdened with a prefrontal cortex that wants someone to *tell them what to do*. Most of the experts now believe that unlimited vacation time puts pressure on employees from all directions. *Internally*

†† Companies that have a yearly expiration date on vacation days and don't allow them to accrue report that 84 percent of employees use all for the allotted time. By contrast, only 48 percent of those working at companies where they can roll over vacation and sick days and get compensated for them when they leave the company or retire use all their time off. If you think that squirreling away unused vacation and sick days can't amount to much money, consider that after a thirty-two-year career, an Orange County, California, employees receive an unused vacation and sick day check for $352,097.34 and that the total financial burden for companies that have to reimburse if those days go unused is estimated in the United States to be $244 billion.

‡‡ *Nudge: Improving Decisions about Health, Wealth, and Happiness.*

§§ *The Paradox of Choice: Why More Is Less.*

and externally. There can be resentment from managers and co-workers if you take off what may be perceived to be "too much" time. Then there's the fact that even though *technically* no one is keeping count of days away from the office, an employee has to wonder if *everyone* is *secretly* counting—and *judging.* And then there is internal fear and guilt that just maybe taking the "wrong" amount of vacation time will lead to resentment and derail career advancement. It turns out that what our brains want is *less choice and more limits.*

Behavioral science research is populated with a plethora of data from human studies that demonstrate that we can manipulate behavior and change outcomes for the better by adjusting the nature of our "asks," often in minor ways. For example, when researchers added "Every penny will help" to the phrase, "Would you be willing to help by making a donation?" it increased the number of donors to a charity by almost 80 percent. Plus, adding that "low expectation" clause—even pennies matter—not only brought in significantly more donors, those new donors didn't give less because the pennies were mentioned. Researchers also report that by first asking someone for a large request that will likely be turned down, it dramatically increases the chance that a subject will say yes to a more modest second request. (Remember that the next time you go to your boss to ask for a raise.) When we look at the data we have about the *value of constraints* and how *anchoring lower and upper limits* helps both employees and employers get what they want, we can begin to see the flaw in the unlimited vacation time model.

The challenge for managers is to recognize that employee benefits and accommodations are *interconnected* and psychologically *complicated*. But before you throw in the towel and decide that finding and putting into place motivational triggers for your employees in the form of benefit packages and accommodations is too complicated, it's important to remember how critical and productive the small changes we make can be—think Zazie—and the fact that if we *just get it right*, these decisions on employee benefits and accommodations can have a big impact on everything from how hard we have to work as a manager to dollar efficiency, innovation, and creative output.

There is something else critical to remember in all this, as well. Reflect back on Moo.

Everything we did to accommodate the pig was driven by our desire to get what *we* wanted.

So the flip side of this coin—looking at benefits and motivation from the *employee rather than employer* side—is, perhaps, even more interesting. If a film production company is willing to make so many accommodations for an individual piglet, and to do so in a self-serving manner, *employees* should start thinking about how many of their "benefits" are wolves in sheep's clothing that function to serve their *employers* rather than *them*. Consider for a moment car services and expensed meals for employees who work past 9:00 P.M. at Wall Street firms, or the October 2014 announcements by Facebook and Apple that they will help women postpone motherhood by covering the cost of freezing eggs for female employees. Or the fact that IBM announced they will pay for employees to ship breast milk home while nursing mothers are on business trips. Or that a private equity firm announced it would fly nannies and babies with new mothers on business trips for the infant's first year. *If workers stay late working extra hours, what's carfare? As expensive as egg freezing is, maternity leave and attrition costs more. As expensive as it is to ship breast milk or fly nannies, hiring and training new employees is even more expensive.* At first blush, these may seem like nice employee perks. But think about it: *Regardless of how well intentioned they might be,* in the end, *are these accommodations that benefit employees or employer?*

As confusing and overwhelming as all of this is, there *is* a way to get employee benefits and accommodations right. Making accommodations and offering benefits beyond those that are mandated or that are absolutely necessary to attract and retain talent, and that are necessary to allow employees to get their jobs done with comfort and ease, involves looking at benefits and accommodations in terms of three things:

- How we configure our benefit packages impacts motivation.
- Benefits that sound great may not actually *be* great.

And as we're about to see in the next chapter:

- Small often delivers better than big.

Then ask yourself this:

Does what I am offering work alone and *in combination* to propel my workforce to their highest level of accomplishment?

And does what I am doing or what I am offering, individually and in combination, benefit *both* employer and employee?

In other words, *does it increase the tensile strength of my team?* Because the ideal situation is when benefits and accommodations serve both employee *and* employer in a symbiotic, near-perfect relationship of mutual synergistic gain, and while that may take some effort and thought to get right, it's a small fix that will pay off in spades for everyone.

INSIGHT:

Benefit packages and employee accommodations are a big factor in employee motivation, and getting them right is complicated.

Action Steps:
Identify *any specific benefits and accommodations* that can be leveraged to increase employee motivation.

Make sure to identify the *true motivators* and those that *sound good on paper* but *don't actually work* (e.g., identify and eliminate any employee benefits and personal accommodations that either do *nothing* or *function to disengage the workforce*).

Make sure to get the *individual benefits* right and to package them in the right *combinations* as well.

Acknowledge that many accommodations actually serve the *employer* rather than the *employee*.

Use anchors and constraints.

Result:

Higher employee engagement and motivation.

Greater respect for management.

Higher productivity.

Better employee retention rates.

6

BANK EQUITY WITH YOUR LABOR FORCE
★

The Kind That You Can Cash In Later

Case Study:
The film *Going in Style*. Warner Bros. Directed by Martin
Brest; starring George Burns, Art Carney, and Lee Strasberg.

WHAT IF AN actress playing the lead in your movie approaches
you when you're shooting on location in Memphis, Tennessee, and
asks for a few days off to go home to Los Angeles to see her
daughter? The schedule is complex, and she's in virtually every
scene—which means that even if you want to give her a few days
off, and even if you could move the schedule around and make it
work without impacting the budget, it might backfire if, for some
reason, she doesn't make it back on time. Furthermore, if you do
accommodate her, then other cast members are apt to make similar requests. *Everyone* wants time off to see their kids. *Everyone*
wants more time and larger departmental budgets, more equipment, and more manpower. In fact, as a manager, you are fielding

requests like these *every day* from *every direction*, and your first instinct is likely a resounding, universal no to all of them. After all, that actress is well paid and under contract—daughter or no daughter, those departmental budgets are set, and manpower and equipment were agreed on in preproduction.

Now expand this management dilemma beyond the film business and beyond *specific asks*. How about *broad issues* and *policy*? Say you're the manager of a manufacturing company; do you keep the spare parts under lock and key? *After all, they are valuable and could be stolen.* Or imagine that you're a floor manager at a factory; do you check exit times against individual time cards? The guys *could* be hitting you up for overtime they didn't really earn. As a manager, you are well within your rights to say "No," to police, and to guard—not only spare parts but also assets like time. In fact, *it's your job to do these things*. The question is, *should you*?

The answer is, *maybe not*. And here's why:

These day-to-day "asks" and "tone-setting" management decisions, if handled correctly, present an opportunity to build equity with the workforce that works to build tensile strength and motivation even beyond what is accomplished by the structural elements of the Oscar Effect and the coordinated accommodations and benefit packages you already offer.

Building equity often involves saying yes when you think you shouldn't. It begins as a relationship of traded favors that builds off an unspoken *I'll do this for you, you do this for me* and then develops over time into a synergistic, system-wide optimization of assets and talent. When done right, workplace equity can become a reservoir of employee willingness to go above and beyond in a manner that is not always directly *quantifiable* or necessarily even *conscious*. In the best-case scenario, workplace equity is something that accumulates and can be cashed in by both employers and employees when they need it. As valuable as equity is, the data suggests that—on the management side, at least—very few managers build workforce equity *at all*, let alone do it *well*, which is a shame since, as we're about to see, the process of building equity in the workforce and banking a pool of goodwill is *simple to do*. And the reason all managers should give this some thought is that banked equity with the workforce is a soft asset that significantly increases the tensile strength of any organization as it leads to smoother operations, higher employee motivation, greater productivity, maximum efficiency, greater profit, and more creative innovation.

Establishing equity with the labor force is the next step in the tensile strength and employee motivation–building mission and is just as important as establishing trust—but whereas employer/employee trust is a slow build and deep seated, equity is more direct and transactional—at least to start. Ironically, *building equity* involves *being equitable*. And if there is one undeniable truth of management that I've learned over many years, it's that everyone wants to be treated fairly—and employees know *instantly* when they are, or are not, being treated with both professional and personal respect and a sense of fair play.

The reason this matters so much is that a *lack* of workplace equity first erodes trust, loyalty, and respect and then begins to cripple efficiency, diminish productivity, and undermine creativity and innovation, and it invariably leads to a loss of power as it decreases motivation and engagement. In the worst-case scenario, it can destroy a business. *Without equity, a manager may have warm bodies doing the bare minimum but nobody who will go the extra mile.*

I was lucky enough to have learned this lesson early in my career on *Going in Style*, a Martin Brest film shot in 1979 with comedic legends George Burns and Art Carney and the great Lee Strasberg. I have all sorts of fond memories from that picture and a few not so fond, but I'll tell you one of the good stories first. I was young, and the cast was old, and I knew that I was getting my feet wet in the business with a few of the greats. One day, I asked George Burns—who was a spry, sharp-witted, cigar-smoking, martini-drinking eighty-three at the time—to tell my brother, Phil, who was on set visiting me on a break from medical school, some doctor jokes. He obliged, and an hour later when I returned to his dressing room, Phil was still there laughing, and George was still going strong. Add Art Carney to the mix—Ed Norton from *The Honeymooners*—and on set it was nonstop stand-up; Art didn't have an off switch, either. *Going in Style* was one of the first features I ever worked on, and in many ways it was a christening by the comedic greats of a bygone era.

Now for one of the not-so-fond memories.

Early on, when we were shooting on the stage at Kaufman Astoria Studios in Queens, the production manager told me—the new guy with little experience and few established relationships—to stand at the door when we wrapped and record exactly what time each crew member left for the day. The crew was on a flat rate for eight hours, but, as we commonly do, we had gone into overtime that day. The thing of it was, even though each crew member would record his or her hours on an official weekly time card, my boss wanted me to verify everyone's accuracy.

To say that this tactic didn't go over well would be an egregious understatement. By putting someone at the door with a clipboard and a watch, management may have been well within their rights, but they were saying loud and clear to the entire crew, *we don't trust you.* Luckily for me, when the guys started giving me a hard time, the key grip, Jimmy Finnerty, told them to knock it off. He recognized—and made it clear—that I was just doing what I was told to do, which saved me but not the production manager.

As I was standing there that day, at first I was thinking only one thing: *This isn't going to end well.* Then I started thinking about how easy it is to get all the *big things* in management *right* and then get the *small things* terribly *wrong*, and how that can completely derail authority and the ability to lead and manage. I was about to learn something that I would go on to say to people over and over again during my career: that, first and foremost, "being a good manager involves keeping what is a very delicate balance of power between employer and employees in check" and that "the balance of power between management and employees has to be at equilibrium, or the entire system can fail."

At one o'clock the next day, by flexing some union muscle, the crew made an aggressive move to reestablish that equilibrium. Union rules state that when we're shooting, the company has to break for a one-hour meal every six hours. There are three additional stipulations: First, if a catered meal isn't provided, the crew has to be given meal money. Second, they have to be allotted what is called "walking time," which means that a reasonable amount of time has to be added to that mealtime hour for the crew to get to and from a restaurant. And third, the unspecified but understood part of the contract is that there has to be at least one "acceptable restaurant" close by—for example, a deli or a fast-food restaurant would not be acceptable.*

There's never an argument over meal money—it's pretty generous and set by union contract. As for walking time, that's pretty straightforward, too—particularly if we are shooting in an area like New York City that has lots of restaurants. Typically, we just add ten minutes to the lunch hour and everyone is happy. On the other hand, the subjective nature of the term *acceptable restaurant* can work against management if the crew decides to demonstrate the collective power they actually have.

When we broke for lunch the day following the "*we don't trust you/clipboard incident*," the shop steward quietly informed the production manager that there were no acceptable restaurants close to where we were shooting that day. The production manager essentially had a wildcat work stoppage on her hands and immediately went ballistic, and then, because she knew she had no choice, she scrambled to arrange for a couple of buses to take the eighty-person crew to what they deemed to be an acceptable restaurant.

As you can imagine, that took some time.

What should have been a one-hour-plus-ten-minute meal that day ended up taking over three hours. Even prorated in 1979 film production dollars, that was one hell of an expensive lunch. I'm

---

* These rules are complicated and nuanced. For example, if there is only one acceptable restaurant and it can only seat forty people at a time, if we have a seventy-man crew, the meal period wouldn't be over until one hour after the last man is seated.

relating this story here because it's a stellar example of how to *not build equity with the workforce*, and as we're about to see, as direct a lesson as this was, the expensive lunch may have only been the tip of the iceberg.

Here's why:

That lunch was only the part of the loss that was identifiable and quantifiable.

Managers are often paid back for the actions they take—or don't take—in ways that can't be directly measured or that they may not even be aware of. I've witnessed time and again situations where a single perception of lack of fairness by an employee derails engagement, slows productivity, and sends creative idea generation and innovation into shutdown. The last thing a manager wants is for the mind-set of employees to be, *I'll do my job, but I'm not going to do anything beyond the bare minimum to help here.* Other times, the payback may not even be conscious on the part of the employees—it just manifests as disengaged, not-too-happy-here, productivity-busting malaise.

While I've found that the perception of even a small slight becomes personal and a matter of principle very quickly and erodes the functionality of a team as it diminishes output, the data to support this observation is comprehensive. The American Psychological Association (APA) found that 93 percent of employees who felt valued by management reported that they were motivated to do their very best for their employer. Yet only 33 percent of those who *didn't feel valued* by their employers reported the same level of workplace commitment. And it gets worse. The APA also reports that 80 percent of employees who are dissatisfied with their *direct manager* are disengaged at work.

As counterintuitive as it may be, this is good news:

It means that control over employee engagement and equity building lies with *management*, not with *employees*.
And that means a manager has the power to *fix* it.

The downside of *not* building goodwill reaches even further. Gallup found a significant correlation between levels of employee engagement at work and the level of self-reported creative idea generation,[†] which means that lack of engagement not only directly impacts productivity and efficiency but also likely impacts creativity and innovation. Since creative ideas are the foundation for innovation, employee engagement is something managers should want to cultivate, and a surefire way to disengage your workforce and create a string of cascading inefficiencies is to fail to build equity with your team.

I learned a powerful lesson standing at the studio door checking times that day on *Going in Style*—one that has been reinforced many times over the years. And that lesson wasn't just about the power of employees or unions or the reckless nature of the sometimes-stupid decisions made by management. It was this:

It's almost always the small things—not the big things—that matter when building equity in relationships.

Why? Because the "big things"—salary, fringe benefits, job title, and so on—are often viewed as "*corporate policy*," while it's the small, *personal things* that are measures of integrity, honesty,

---

[†] Fifty-nine percent of "engaged employees" agreed with the statement "*my job brings out my most creative ideas*," versus only 17 percent of employees who are "not engaged," versus only 3 percent of completely disengaged employees.

intent, and a sense of fair play that at the end of the day build equity with employees.[‡]

I've seen managers on film sets make this same type of mistake time and again. A company might be hiring world-class people and spending tens of millions of dollars on the production, including high salaries and top-notch fringe benefits, and then make terrible small decisions over what would amount to nickels and dimes. In so doing, without even knowing it, management is derailing the power they have to cultivate a strong, motivated team, and it ends up being costly in ways they may never know. The transportation coordinator on an out-of-town film who is asked by management to move from a great hotel to a good one to save twenty bucks a day is someone who controls a budget in excess of a million dollars. *You don't want him pissed off.* Yet I've seen managers repeatedly make foolish, penny-wise decisions that insult and offend and disengage—forgetting perhaps that the people we manage have the option of pointing out all those extra half-second inefficiencies and creative insights that can impact profit, or they can look the other way and do what is required but nothing more.

Consider for a moment a small change in management code and the potential impact it can have on outcomes. Imagine if instead of clocking "out times" at the door of the studio on *Going in Style* that telegraphed *we don't trust you*, management had

---

[‡] As noted in the previous chapter, this is supported by a plethora of behavioral research on intrinsic motivation, including the previously mentioned work of Harry F. Harlow, Richard M. Ryan, Edward L. Deci, Abraham Maslow, and also Frederick Herzberg, who found that such factors as salary, fringe benefits, and working conditions are important on a basic level but don't motivate workers as much as our internal drives (e.g., self-actualization).

instead had a representative at the door with a small gesture that said, *we appreciate your effort*—say, shaking hands as the guys left for the day? On *The Wanderers*, one of my first movies, Fred Caruso, the production manager, told me an anecdote about Dino De Laurentiis (producer of *Ragtime*, *La Strada*, and numerous others) bringing coffee to the dolly grip and assistant cameraman on a bitterly cold night shoot because they couldn't leave the camera. When the legendary producer Saul Zaentz (*The English Patient*, *One Flew Over the Cuckoo's Nest*) was making *Amadeus* (1983) in Prague in the dead of winter, he came by the set and noticed that the American crew were decked out in Eddie Bauer goose down parkas, ski pants, and heavy boots, while the local Hungarian crew members were attired in blue jeans and threadbare jackets as they worked in subfreezing temperatures. Without saying a word to anyone, the next day he had his assistant order one hundred sets of heavy winter gear in varying sizes and had them shipped in immediately. Dick Quinlan, the gaffer on the film and a good friend of mine, told me the crew was dumbstruck by the gesture and that when the clothing was distributed, some of the men had tears in their eyes. Gestures like these in an industry where a couple of buses and two hours of missed time in a shooting day can run tens of thousands of dollars can go a long way toward building goodwill that is almost guaranteed to be paid back at some point in the future. And this is true in every business, not just in filmmaking.

Companies across industries have found that it is often the small perks that don't cost a company much that are most appreciated by employees, build the most equity, and drive success over time. The companies with summer hours that require employees to come in a half hour early five days a week so they can leave at 1:00 P.M. on Fridays only lose thirty minutes of real work time each week, yet the difference in banked equity and workplace happiness is palpable. Facebook and Google report that, with a few exceptions, many of the great employee perks they are known for and that give them equity with their workforce are the ones that actually cost the company next to nothing—ATMs in the lobby, dry cleaning pickup and drop-off available at work, flexible work hours, and the like. These efforts show respect and say *we're thinking about you and trying to make your life easier* (not to mention keeping employees at work—not ducking out to do errands).

Bob Chapman, the CEO of the $2 billion global capital equipment and engineering consulting firm Barry-Wehmiller, reported that he turned HayssenSandiacre, a South Carolina manufacturing company, around by finding ways to show respect to employees in numerous small ways, including by making them feel that management felt they were trustworthy. By the time he bought the company, employee morale had bottomed out, and he cited the fact that the spare parts the workers needed to do their jobs were kept in a locked cage, and retrieving them not only took more time than necessary, it made the employees feel that management felt they weren't trustworthy and might steal—so he immediately changed that. Similarly, when Douglas Conant took over as CEO of Campbell's, he began the process of turning that company around, not with a big change like raising salaries but with a small gesture—he wrote a handwritten letter of thanks to all thirty thousand employees.

As you might have guessed, I wasn't recording names and out times at the wrap after that three-hour lunch on *Going in Style*, and the issue of acceptable restaurants never came up again. But at that point, it hardly mattered. The damage had been done.

Years later when I was working on the film *City by the Sea*, I relied on building up and then cashing in *a lot* of equity when we had six weeks of night shooting in January and February on the waterfront of the Jersey Shore. The call was at 4:00 P.M. every day, and we worked outside in the brutal cold until the wrap at 4:00 A.M. when we headed back to local hotels to try to get some sleep during the daylight hours. The temperature averaged fifteen degrees at night, and with the windchill, it hovered around zero. As bad as the freezing cold was, the conditions were also dangerous and technically challenging, as well. The boardwalk was icy and in disrepair—actress Patti LuPone's foot actually went through some boards, and she injured her ankle—equipment froze, and the howling wind made recording sound difficult. As a manager, it's not easy to motivate a workforce to tackle their jobs with enthusiasm and professionalism in such a debilitating environment—*even when that workforce is highly motivated to begin with*. It's even harder to hold a workforce to *peak performance* and *tight deadlines* in such tough working conditions—especially when many of those jobs are physically grueling and/or creatively demanding. So I made sure that even though I was managing the crew and making tough decisions about money and time, I remembered to take care of the small things by showing respect for how hard everyone was working. I knew that having a pocket full of equity to cash in would take me a long way—and it did.

That day at the studio door on *Going in Style* taught me the value of adding fifteen minutes to the dinner hour on *City by the Sea* so the crew could thaw out and warm up. I brought in additional space heaters and heat lamps for the camera department since the camera crew rarely gets to leave the set to defrost, and a lot of the time they can't even wear gloves because they need their fingers for endless meticulous mechanical work—from changing film, batteries, and lenses to operating a zoom gun. By repeatedly doing small things that demonstrated *consideration*, when *I* needed something above and beyond from the crew, I was more likely to get it. Say the director of photography and director decide to alter a shot at 2:00 A.M.—maybe shifting the camera angle by thirty degrees, which might necessitate an hour-long move of man-lifts, cranes, lights, and cables that the guys have spent two or three hours to set up already. I want professionalism, enthusiasm, hustle, and creative solutions applied to that task, not sluggish, disgruntled employees.

Of equal importance, I try to accommodate the cast as well as the crew in certain circumstances. Kate Beckinsale was the actress in Memphis on *Nothing But the Truth* who asked me if I could adjust the schedule to give her a four-day weekend so she could go home to see her daughter in Los Angeles. It would have been easy to say no. We had a complex schedule, and Kate was in most of the scenes in the movie, which meant that with her not there, we had little flexibility. But I knew that as much as there was a downside to letting her go, there was an upside, too. By flipping a few days around on the schedule in a way that didn't have a significant financial impact, I was able to accommodate her—and I knew that banked *me* some equity. For instance, if I needed to give her an unusually early call so I could accommodate someone else, I knew she would be on board with it. Then, of course, there are the less-direct immeasurables; for instance, how does feeling respected and taken care of pay back in creative performance?

Some production managers make it a point of showing up at 3:00 A.M. on a night shoot with boxes of pizza or Chinese food at the wrap, and even though we get meal money or catered meals and all-day access to food, *that means something*. I make it a point to schedule easier, straight, eight-hour days for Fridays and set a 6:00 A.M. call to get the crew home as early as possible so they can get a jump on the weekend. These kinds of small considerations pay off in spades.

On the film *Quick Change* when we were about to wrap at 4:30 A.M. after filming a night sequence at Newark International Airport[§], Bill Murray and codirector Howard Franklin came up with one final, additional shot they wanted to make. A close-up would have been one thing, but what they envisioned was a forty-foot dolly shot crossing the terminal that would involve close to one hundred extras and the camera looking east through ceiling-to-floor glass. To get the shot, we needed it to still be (relatively) dark outside, and sunrise was at 4:48—*eighteen minutes away*. With the sun so close to rising and blowing the take, the decision to go forward had to be swift and definitive. Mike Chapman, the director of photography, was adamant; there wasn't enough time. The sun would be streaming through the window before we could even roll a single take.

I thought we had a decent chance. I calculated that if we hauled ass, we just might get the shot, and since Bill really wanted to go for it, if we pulled it off, this was a chance for me, as well as the crew, to build some equity with him. But I didn't just *tell the*

§ Name changed to *Newark Liberty International Airport* in 2002.

crew what we wanted to do; I *asked them* their opinion by quickly assembling a handful of the key department heads and posing the questions, "What do you think? Can you pull it off?" This was a strategic decision that cost me a few minutes but likely changed the outcome because it showed professional respect. I was asking these men and women, who had already worked a tough twelve-hour night and still had another hour or more to load trucks and then an hour's drive home, to kill themselves in order to get one more shot. Selfishly, any one of the department heads could have said, "No, there isn't enough time," and they would have been at least eighteen minutes closer to going home. But they didn't; to a man, they said, "Let's go for it."

Immediately, everybody kicked it up a notch, a few normal protocols were ignored, and every department began working simultaneously and at high speed. The dolly track was laid, the camera mounted, I staged the ninety extras in less than ten minutes, and we were able to get three takes in before the sun blasted through the wall of windows. And I got a handshake and a thank-you from Bill Murray as we wrapped as I in turn was shaking hands with and thanking the crew.

In a situation like this, as a manager, I know that I have a lot going for me—segmented jobs and incremental tasks, trust, the Oscar Effect, *and* banked equity, as well. The crew wants to look good, be recommended for future jobs, and be part of a great project, and they want to prove they can do anything and go the distance. But in the end, effort of this magnitude only happens when a manager has banked a pool of equity with the workforce. At 4:30 A.M. after a long night, it's *really* easy to find a way to say no to additional work.

Over the years, I have found some very specific equity-building strategies—beyond the common sense of handshakes, thank-yous, hot food, and reasonable, thoughtful accommodations. *And the best part is that they cost the company absolutely nothing and are simple to code into day-to-day team management.*

For starters . . .

DEMOCRATIZE THE PLAYING FIELD AS MUCH AS POSSIBLE.

A common sentiment on set when the going gets tough is, "We're all in this together." And it's true. Even though there is great variance in title, power, and salary on a film set, when it's fifteen degrees out, it's fifteen degrees for everyone, even if your name is Robert De Niro or James Franco. We don't have a top floor with C-suites. When the wind was howling and the crew was in high-tech, cold-weather gear on *City by the Sea*, James Franco was out there, too—in a T-shirt and light jacket. Because we are in this together and that's evident, there is an atmosphere of camaraderie that goes a long way toward building equity.

The key is to take *that* concept and run with it. For instance, I make sure that if the electricians are hauling cable and setting lights at 3:00 A.M. with a biting wind and pelting sleet, I'm standing right there out in the elements, too—even when I don't need to be. That makes me easy to find if they have a question, and that goes a long way toward building equity with the crew that I can cash in later. And when we wrap with a crew in overtime, I don't have someone at the door double-checking out times. Instead, I'm there saying, "Thanks for a great day, everybody. Safe home."

RESPECT INDIVIDUAL DIFFERENCES.

One brutal night on *City by the Sea* when I finally broke the crew at midnight for "lunch," I headed into our nearby office to thaw out. As I was pulling off my ice-encrusted parka, I noticed what appeared to be a homeless guy asleep under one of the desks. As I was trying to decide what to do, he lifted his head up off the floor, opened his eyes, and turned toward me, and I realized that it wasn't a homeless guy at all—it was James Franco who played the drug-addicted, homeless son of Vincent LaMarca (played by Robert De Niro in the film), staying in character. I laughed, partly out of relief that I wasn't facing an encounter with some poor guy who just wanted in from the cold, and partly because I found it amusing that there were actors who could slip into character on command and without much prep and others who stayed in character even when we weren't shooting. As a manager, it's vital to recognize that *everyone does things differently*. In order to succeed, you have to allow for those individual differences and accept the fact that you have to manage *different* people *differently*.

The good news is that I've learned over the years that *respect for process and individuality* will build equity fast. Why? Because it makes a statement—it says, "I trust and respect your professionalism even if *I* would do this task differently." And that can lead to creative freedom and innovation that improves the quality of what you are doing. On the Penny Marshall film *Big* when we were shooting a corporate party scene with Tom Hanks (playing Josh Baskin the twelve-year-old in a grown-up body), he began eating miniature ears of baby corn from the buffet table by nibbling the kernels the way one would with a regular-size ear. The scene was not scripted that way, and it proved to be a hysterical improv moment in the film. As a manager, you want all your employees to have that freedom to express those great, unscripted moments of genius—and an environment that respects individuality allows that to happen.

TRADE FAVORS IN A JUDICIOUS AND SELF-SERVING MANNER.

I've found that by listening to the problems and requests of individual department heads and then, when it's appropriate, going to bat for them to satisfy *their needs*, I can build equity in a way that *looks* gratuitous but in the end is often *self-serving*.

Say that a makeup artist comes to me because he or she would like an additional staff member for a week because of some nuance during that shooting period—maybe we have a lot of extras or rain scenes or complicated special effects that week. By approving that hire,** I've built equity with the makeup department by alleviating their workload and stress *and also indirectly built equity with the director and producers* because there now is a greater chance that we will make our day's work and not fall behind. And at the same time that I'm building equity, I'm also increasing the tensile strength of my team by communicating to the makeup department that I value their individual contributions. I am acknowledging that I understand that the job of making the cast

---

** With production costs running $20,000 an hour, hiring an extra pair of hands for the week is a nominal cost if it saves us time.

look good and feel relaxed is very important to the creative process and shouldn't be rushed.

And here's the poetic beauty: in each case of the building up and then cashing in of equity, my stock rises in the eyes of the crew, the crew's stock rises in my eyes, my stock simultaneously rises in the eyes of the director and producers, and each movie ends up being better for it. In other words, the give-and-take comes full circle as it increases our overall tensile strength as an organization *and* improves our productivity and the quality of our creative output.

AS WITH EVERYTHING YOU DO AS A MANAGER, THIS HAS TO BE *AUTHENTIC* AND *GENUINE*.

If a manager who is perceived as unreasonable and disrespectful brings in a few boxes of doughnuts on a late-night shoot, it will look like just what it is—a transparent attempt to mollify an unhappy workforce with a few dollars' worth of food. A move like that can actually worsen the situation, as the takeaway for employees becomes, *How stupid does he or she think we are?* The flip side, of course, is that when a gesture like that is perceived to be *in character* and *genuinely* reflective of management's appreciation of the workforce, it can solidify those feelings of mutual appreciation and professional respect as it builds equity you are going to need in the future. This observation is backed up by outside data, as well. According to Bersin & Associates, companies with serious employee recognition programs are "12 times more likely to have strong business results," and yet only 20 percent of companies manage to have programs like this in place.

THE LITMUS TEST AND END GOAL? THOSE COVETED,
TEAM-WIDE, "I AM SPARTACUS" MOMENTS.

In the Stanley Kubrick film *Spartacus* (1960), starring Kirk Douglas, the slave army that has been brutally defeated by a Roman general is told that their lives will be spared if they identify and hand over their leader, Spartacus, for crucifixion. As Spartacus stands up to identify himself in order to save his men, Antoninus, the slave sitting on his right (played by Tony Curtis) also stands, and the two men simultaneously declare, "I am Spartacus." The other slaves instantly follow suit, and in a dramatic display of loyalty to protect their leader, one by one all of them step forward and declare, "I am Spartacus," as well.

On many of the films I have worked on, there have been a number of "I am Spartacus" moments, and they are seminal events for the crew for several reasons. When we are shooting and something goes wrong, tension can get high. If a stressed-out director demands to know whose fault something is—say, what's causing a delay—if we have a cohesive crew, a few people who had nothing to do with the problem will invariably mumble, "My fault." That usually quickly gains momentum as more people volunteer to take the blame until it culminates with a crew member declaring, "I am Spartacus." On top of generating laughter and defusing a tense situation, this communicates to the director that as much as the crew is working for him or her, they are first and foremost a team. When I take the fall by saying, "It's my fault"—as I often do—it has a similar impact. The crew member whose fault it *really* is—and most on the crew know who that is—is grateful to have his back covered. The other crew members are now assured that if they screw up—and they may—they will be protected, as well. This makes a statement about the power inherent in a large, cohesive group—like a flock of birds or a school of fish—*we understand that an individual can be slaughtered easily, but there is protection in the group*.

In this Kirk Douglas movie, it ends badly for everyone—the loyalty results in the Roman general killing every one of the soldiers in order to be assured that he has indeed killed Spartacus. But our stressed-out director is usually smart enough to know that he can't berate the entire crew. So when I hear "I am Spartacus" on the set, it indicates to me that we have achieved a high degree of tensile strength and we are a unified team with collective, aggregate, palpable, bankable equity, and that means without question that we have the greatest chance for success with the project—both financially and creatively.

INSIGHT:

Banking equity with your labor force functions as a valuable soft asset.

Action Steps:
Understand that small gestures often mean more than big ones.
Democratize the playing field.
Respect individual differences.
Trade favors in a judicious and self-serving manner.
Be *authentic* and *genuine*.
Create team-wide "I am Spartacus" moments.

Result:

Cohesion and reciprocity.

Improved relationship between management and work-force.

Increased productivity and creative output.

7

OPTIMIZE AND EXPLOIT DIVERSITY

WHAT DO A US CONSTITUTIONAL LAW SCHOLAR,
PRISON GUARDS, AND A GIRLS' SOCCER TEAM
HAVE IN COMMON?

CASE STUDY:
The film *Nothing But the Truth*. Yari Film Group. Directed by
Rod Lurie; starring Kate Beckinsale, Matt Dillon, Vera
Farmiga, and Alan Alda.

IN ANSWER TO the above question, other than the fact that they
were all working together on a film set, just about nothing—and
that's a good thing. In fact, a close examination of diversity in filmmaking offers some compelling insight into why other businesses
should make sure that they are as diverse as possible and in all possible ways—from race and gender to experience and skill set—
and not simply because it is the equitable thing to do.

And here's why:

*There is an abundance of data that demonstrates that a diverse
workforce leads to higher profit, greater innovation, and more stable
companies.*

This stems in part from the fact that *homogeneous groups are more likely to engage in homogeneous thinking and fall victim to groupthink*—which limits innovation—while a diversity of minds and skill sets results in more creative—and profitable—insights.* Think of it this way: if a group of twenty-five-year-old, college-educated, white, male marketing managers with similar upbringings and education get together to solve a problem—substitute any homogeneous group you want here—they will likely approach that problem with similar skill sets and perspectives. And data shows that since they think very similarly, they are more likely to arrive at a less innovative solution to that problem than a more diverse group would.

To put it in coding terms, the more limited the diversity of your team, the more likely you will suffer from a "garbage in / garbage out"—or worse yet, "garbage in / gospel out"—type of result.† But this phenomenon is more complex than the obvious and linear, *if-you-limit-what-you-put-in, you-limit-what-you-get-out* type of equation might predict. Here's why: if you happen to be one of those homogeneous marketing managers, you will *notice the broad similarities in your group and behave accordingly.* Which includes *not trying as hard.*

People in groups where participants are very similar not only

---

* *Groupthink* is a term that was first coined in 1972 by Irving L. Janis in his book *Victims of Groupthink: A Psychological Study of Foreign-Policy Decisions and Fiascoes.* He defined it as the "psychological drive for consensus at any cost that suppresses dissent and appraisal of alternatives in cohesive decision making groups."

† *Garbage in / garbage out* is an old computer term reminding us that if what we input is flawed, we won't get high-quality output. *Garbage in / gospel out* refers to how we often blindly believe whatever a computer gives us regardless of quality, simply because a computer search makes it look official.

arrive with like mind-sets, orientations, and tools, but they also don't work as hard as they do when they are in groups that are more heterogeneous—in part because they anticipate that *they don't have to. And they're right in that assessment.* In the absence of differing ideas and opinions, members of a group with little or no diversity aren't challenged very much during the process of problem-solving.

Researchers have found that diverse groups work harder, are more open-minded and, in the end, develop more innovative solutions.

And there are complex cognitive, social, and behavioral mechanisms at work that allow this to happen. For starters, the collective similarity of group members fosters *confirmation bias*—seeking out information that confirms what we already think—and *anchoring*—hanging tight to our initial impressions going into a situation. In fact, there is evidence that simply *being aware* that the people around us *may* have a different perspective than we do sets us up to be more open, more inquisitive, and more willing to prepare. Therefore, people in homogeneous groups collectively not only *arrive* with less and do less work but also *leave* with less in terms of creative output and solutions, as well. As a result, I have always looked at putting together a team as analogous to putting together a toolbox. If I have the option, I include the widest variety of different tools as possible. In other words, *I don't fill the whole thing with, say, just hammers.*

Since we know that diversity is good for business, having a diverse workplace and diverse teams has become, particularly of late, a top corporate goal. One that, admittedly, many industries and companies fail to achieve—and for a whole lot of complex interconnected reasons, the most insidious of which may be this:

Social scientists have found that as good as diversity is for innovation and profit, it can also make us feel *uncomfortable*, so we often revert to the mean—*our mean*—and hire people similar to ourselves.

Which of course circles us right back to the fact that *when we limit our inputs, we limit our outputs*. In other words, when it comes to diversity, we self-sabotage.

While diversity comes in many forms—from race, gender, age, nationality, religion, life experience, education, skill set, and talent to expertise, philosophical orientation, cultural background, political orientation, and worldview—race and gender tend to be the diversity metrics most companies look at when they are looking at staff composition and hiring practices. And as we are about to see—from both my experience and from industry data—when it comes to diversity of things like talent, expertise, and skill set, the film industry is highly diverse and benefits enormously because of it. But when it comes to diversity of race and gender, as we are also about to see, the film industry falls miserably short. In fact, as much as I have worked day in and day out on film sets with people from all walks of life who have a wide diversity of *skill set*, *experience*, and *cultural and professional perspective*, the enormous value add-on that this type of diversity provides is tragically undermined by an *extreme lack of diversity when it comes to race and gender*. And the film business isn't the only industry with gender and race imbalances.

THE TECH INDUSTRY has long been criticized for a lack of gender and racial diversity. Laszlo Bock, Google's senior vice president of People Operations, reports that Google employees are

70 percent male, 61 percent white, 30 percent Asian, 3 percent Hispanic, and 2 percent black. Which means that when compared to the general population, males and Asians are *overrepresented*, and women, blacks, and Hispanics are dramatically *underrepresented*. As skewed as these numbers are, in many ways it's a miracle that they're not worse. And here's why:

Fewer than 20 percent of all college degrees are earned by blacks and Hispanics, and of those degrees, fewer than 10 percent are with a major in computer science.‡ Women fall short, as well, earning only 18 percent of computer science degrees despite the fact that women represent more than half of all college graduates. What this means is that finding and recruiting minorities and women—let alone black or Hispanic *women*—with a degree in computer science who are a good fit for a particular tech company and who actually *want* the job (industry culture, as well as pipeline are both issues in hiring and retaining women and minorities in tech) is sort of like finding the computer science needle in the college-recruiting haystack.

As hard as the tech industry is trying to improve their diversity numbers,§ and as much as they have been criticized for not

---

‡ Looking at top schools in the field only, Computing Research Association reports that in 2013, 4.5 percent of all new recipients of bachelor's degrees in computer science or computer engineering were earned by African Americans and 6.5 percent by Hispanics. Looking at computer science graduates at a broader base of colleges and universities, the National Center for Education Statistics found that blacks and Hispanics each made up about 9 percent of graduates in 2012.

§ Just as a single example, Google has spent over $40 million to bring computer science education to women and girls and sent an engineer to Howard University to work on improving the computer science curriculum.

doing more—like recruiting employees from more ethnically diverse colleges and making the culture of Silicon Valley more welcoming to "outsiders"—tech firms like Google have a diversity problem caused to a large degree by a *math problem*. It's not necessarily that tech companies don't value diversity; it's that achieving it can be a losing game of percentages.

But while the tech industry has a diversity problem that stems at least to some degree from a lack of *availability* of diverse talent,** the film industry—which posts *far worse diversity numbers than tech does* when it comes to women and is on a miserable par with the tech industry when it comes to minorities—got to its racial and gender disparity via a *different* type of math problem.

The Directors Guild of America (DGA)†† reports that in 2015, only 14 percent of its members listed as directors were women. Of directors who were members of the DGA, 3.6 percent were African American, 2.7 percent Latinos, and 1.9 percent Asian Americans. And that's just the breakdown of DGA *membership*—it doesn't account for how often any of these women or minority directors actually got *hired*.

This means that 86 percent of US film and television directors in the DGA are men, a tiny fraction of whom are members of a minority. When you index these numbers against the total US population, which is 50.8 percent female, 13.2 percent African

---

** *USA Today* reported that minority computer science majors graduate at twice the rate they are being hired, which points to the need for a change in recruitment policies.

†† The DGA is the labor organization that represents directors and directorial team members (assistant directors, stage managers, et al.) and has contracts with the major studios and producing entities. Membership is required in the DGA to get hired to direct a big studio picture or network/cable signatory television show.

American, 17.4 percent Latinos, and 5.4 percent Asian American, you begin to see the scope of the underrepresentation of women and minorities in the higher echelons of filmmaking.

With such a small pool of available women and minority directors to pull from, you might think that they would have a good chance of getting *hired*. Simple supply and demand. Right?

Wrong.

Not only are women and minorities in short *supply*, they are in short *demand*, too, and not just in feature films but in television production, as well.

In the 2014 television season, of the 3,900 episodes produced, white women directed only 13 percent (507 episodes), minority men directed 15 percent (585 episodes), and only 3 percent (117 episodes) were directed by minority women, which left a whopping 69 percent of all episodic TV in the hands of white male directors (2,691 episodes).

When you look at the industry-wide data, the systemic white-male dominance in feature film and television reaches all the way from higher-ups at the studios—who are making the deals and controlling the money—to the talent agencies representing writers, directors, and actors to the DGA and the Academy of Motion Picture Arts and Sciences, which is roughly 77 percent male and 94 percent white. Which means that the deck is stacked in favor of white men from the conception of a project to Oscar Night—or, to put it metaphorically, it's an industry with a toolbox full of hammers.

Just like in tech, while there has been some progress in recent years in improving "equal opportunity employment," and there are numerous industry programs directed toward nurturing women and minority talent,[‡‡] during more than three decades working on over fifty feature films, I can only recall working with one black location manager, one black assistant director, and one black teamster, and he was "shaping the hall," which means that he didn't have "a book"—or union card—but was allowed to work because there were more drivers needed at that time than the union had members. Women in the grip, electric, teamster, and construction departments were almost unheard of, while, in a very 1950s-gender-stereotyped way, women populated the makeup, hair, and wardrobe departments along with the office staff. The way the math breaks down—and ignoring any television I did and dealing only with my feature film projects—over my career, out of (give or take) fifty A-list feature film projects, I worked with forty-six white male directors.

That's a staggering 92 percent.

I only worked with two minority directors—Michael Schultz (African American) on *The Last Dragon* and Alfonso Cuarón (Mexican) on *Great Expectations*.

Thirty-year career. One black director. One (foreign-born, not American) Latino director.

To be fair, I did have the privilege of working with two women directors—but *only* two. Barbra Streisand on her acclaimed film *The Prince of Tides* (nominated for seven Academy Awards), and Penny Marshall on *Big*—nominated for two Academy Awards

---

[‡‡] CBS Directing Initiative, Disney | ABC Directing Program, Fox Global Directors Initiative, HBOAccess Program, NBCUniversal Directing Fellowship, Sony Pictures Television Diverse Directors Program, Viacom Media Networks Spectrum Director Development Program, Warner Bros. Emerging Film Directors Workshop, and others.

and the first film directed by a woman *to gross over $100 million in US box office receipts.*

Fifty projects, 4 percent *of which were directed by women.*[§§]

But before you decide that the only thing wrong with that short list of women is its length, consider for a moment the monumental accomplishments Barbra Streisand and Penny Marshall had achieved *before they got anywhere near a director's chair.* I could list them here, but frankly, it would take up way too many pages. Then consider the staggering recognition these two films received—not just in dollars earned but in critical acclaim as well.

The exclusion of women and minorities in film production is so systemic and institutionalized that from a purely mathematical standpoint, it's staggering. In fact, the problem of exclusion and lack of diversity when it comes to race and gender in film production is so blatant and so absurd that it reminds me of a joke Chris Rock—the host of the Oscars in 2016—told about living in Alpine, New Jersey, in *Kill the Messenger.*

> In my neighborhood, there are four black people. Hundreds of houses, four black people. Who are these black people? Well, there's me, Mary J. Blige, Jay-Z, and Eddie Murphy. Only black people in the whole neighborhood. So let's break it down, let's break it down: me, I'm a decent comedian. I'm a'ight. Mary J. Blige, one of the greatest R&B singers to ever walk the earth.

[§§] If I subtract out seventeen of the eighteen Woody Allen films I did (since they had no chance of being directed by anyone but Woody) and index the two women directors I worked with against thirty-three non-Woody films, that number only inches up to 6 percent.

Jay-Z, one of the greatest rappers to ever live. Eddie Murphy, one of the funniest actors to ever, ever do it . . .

Do you know what the white man who lives next door to me does for a living? He's a fucking dentist! He ain't the best dentist in the world . . . he ain't going to the dental hall of fame . . .

See, the black man gotta fly to get to somethin' the white man can walk to. ***

The sad takeaway here is that the exclusionary nature of the film and television industry is such that minorities and women "gotta fly to get to somethin' the white man can walk to."

And before you jump to the conclusion that my sample-of-one career stats may not be representative of the industry, remember that *all the industry data backs up my anecdotal experience.*

THE ISSUE OF diversity in filmmaking is distinct for a number of complex reasons, the first of which is that diversity in filmmaking encompasses two unique but interconnected hiring arenas—*diversity in front of the camera* (cast on-screen) and *the diversity behind it* (production team and crew). Since filmmaking is notoriously predominantly white and male, you can see how that lack of diversity at the top tiers *behind the camera* directly impacts diversity *on-screen*, as well.

Complicating the race- and gender-diversity problem in filmmaking even further is the fact that film is, hands down, the most expensive artistic canvas in the world.

*** Chris Rock, *Kill the Messenger.*

It's *really* hard to get a film made. *For anyone.*

So we're facing a different kind of math problem from the one the tech industry is. And it's not that there is a lack of gender and racially diverse *available talent.* It's that there are so *few jobs,* they're *highly coveted,* talent is hard to assess, and there is no set, proven route to get these jobs like there is in many other fields. To make matters worse for women and minorities, the film industry is stacked from the onset, giving favored status to white men throughout the ranks.

But why should *you* care?

On a macro level, certainly, making sure that there is gender and race equality in employment in any industry is a fair and moral thing to do. And on a micro level, as we know, it's also been proven that having a representative number of women and minorities in an industry, and at a company, leads to more innovation, higher profits, and more stable companies.

But even beyond these compelling factors, *there is another reason that we should care more about the lack of race and gender diversity in film than we do about the lack of diversity in just about any other industry—including tech:*

And that's because race and gender diversity in film and television is far more important than it is in most other fields.

WHILE THE DATA I have presented here illustrates that white men get a disproportionate number of the coveted feature film and episodic television directing jobs—jobs that offer high pay and great benefits—what this also means is that white men are in a position to *choose content (scripts), cast parts, develop characters, and portray issues in a particular light.* In so doing, one segment of the population has disproportionate and unprecedented power to depict social, political, gender, and racial issues *from their (limited) perspectives.* Just as a single example, Barbra Streisand, in addition to winning Oscars, Golden Globes, Grammys, Emmys, and a Tony, received numerous awards and global recognition for all sorts of contributions, *including for her portrayal of women in film.*[†††] Which leads one to wonder what the impact on message and content would be if a more diverse and representative group of people were invited into the conversation. By overpopulating the higher echelons of the film and television industries with white men, it means that white men have more opportunity than other groups (who likely have different perspectives) to shape our culture, make social commentary, and, therefore, effect social change. What this means is that race and gender diversity in filmmaking—in front of and behind the camera—offers more than access to good jobs and high pay. *Many of these jobs also offer access to alter the social conversation.*

And because about half of all film revenue comes from foreign sales, this also means that white men are in a position to portray America and American culture through their lens to the rest of the world. *That* matters in the largest sociopolitical way.

[†††] Just as a few examples: Crystal Apple, City of New York; Woman of Achievement in the Arts; the Women in Film Crystal Award "for outstanding women who, through their endurance and the excellence of their work, have helped to expand the role of women within the entertainment industry": Woman of Courage Award by the National Organization for Women (NOW); the Ordre des Arts et des Lettres; and Breakthrough Awards for "making films that portray women with serious complexity."

One could argue that inequality of access to jobs in film—and other industries that control content and shape culture—leads to a loss of voice that matters far more than does the loss of access to the economic advantages of those coveted jobs.

Just like tech is finding that *new boy network* of gender and race job stereotypes (women and minorities don't go into computer science at the same rate as white and Asian men do, and the industry developed an unwelcoming culture to "outsiders") are hard to battle, the film industry is finding that long-standing, institutionalized *old-boy-network*-style discrimination is hard to dismantle, as well. Which is not to say that we shouldn't be trying a lot harder or that this bias occurs with some organized, premeditated malintent—or that the fix is as simple as, say, quotas. Or to put it another way, all of this would be far *easier* to fix if this skewed diversity was solely a result of overt misogyny and in-your-face racism. Unfortunately, there are other complicating factors and deeply embedded biases at play here, too.

Just as a single example of how gender bias manifests in subtle, insidious ways in American business, when researchers at Wharton, Harvard, and MIT conducted a study that involved playing an audio recording of either a male or a female actor reading identical scripts from a business plan competition, men's pitches beat women's by a two-to-one margin. *Same pitch. Different gender/voice. Radically different outcome.* And this is true even though between 1997 and 2006, businesses fully or majority-owned by women grew at almost twice the rate of all businesses in the United States (42.3 percent versus 23.3 percent).

And it gets worse. In a separate part of that study that involved audio pitches accompanied with (fake) photos of the entrepreneur—some deemed attractive and others unattractive—those who fared the best in getting investors' attention and money were *attractive men*.

Race and gender are, without a doubt, the most visible and measurable—as well as one of the cruelest and most obliquely discriminatory metrics of diversity that we have. But when we look beyond race and gender at other manifestations of diversity in the workplace—diversity of skill set, age, location, job, social status, and professional knowledge and perspective—in that arena, there is no more diverse an environment than a film set. And there is something to learn from this. And that means that aside from all these disappointing statistics and their negative impacts, the film industry has something to offer in terms of insight when it comes to diversity of another sort.

ON FILM PROJECTS, diversity of age, language, ethnicity, culture, religion, education, socioeconomic status, IQ, experience, and skill set covers an enormous spectrum. Don't get me wrong; the fact that we get one side of the *diversity-is-a-good-thing-and-we-go-to-the-ends-of-the-earth-to-achieve-it* equation right in no way compensates for the fact that this is an industry that gets gender and racial inclusion wrong. But it still offers some insight into how to manage diversity of any sort in the workplace.

In filmmaking, we build sets and, for the most part, hire professional actors to play roles. Yet we also frequently choose to shoot in live locations and sometimes use civilians (real people)—say, a butcher, a judge, or city firefighter rather than an actor—to play a role. In other words, *we intentionally choose the challenge and authenticity of diversity over the comfort and ease of uniformity* by shooting at live locations and bringing in "outsiders."

We do it for this reason: it either makes financial sense (it's cheaper to rent a 747 than build one), or it creatively enhances the project (a butcher knows exactly how to "act" like a butcher). And sometimes it accomplishes both—which means lower cost, higher potential revenue, and better art, but—just like with all forms of diversity—it also likely means tougher workplace management.

For example, for me running a film set, a freelance stunt driver who dropped out of high school, an Oscar-winning cinematographer from Germany, a union soundman with a PhD in electrical engineering, a four-year-old child actor, a Serbian fashion model, a makeup artist, and, say, a world-renowned eye surgeon all bring valuable and unique assets to the project. But these diverse individuals need *to be led and managed differently.*

I have to tackle building trust and equity with everyone on set when I'm thrown together with a new and wildly diverse crew—and cast—on every project. I don't have the luxury of reporting to the same office with the same group of coworkers I have known for a decade. I may be filming in France or Italy with French and Italian crews I just met. There may be as many as five different languages spoken on set, and the international labor and union rules are radically different from those in the United States—to say nothing of the cultural differences. When I shot *Sabrina* with Harrison Ford, for instance, we had twenty-three locations in Paris to film at, both an American and a French crew—which included people from Italy, Spain, and the UK— and a unique working environment to adapt to.

We seek out that diversity of expertise close to home, as well. On the film *Nothing But the Truth*, we opted for authenticity for our prison scenes and shot in the Shelby County Correctional Center in Memphis, and we worked with and cast real Tennessee prison guards, US marshals, and a federal judge. This meant that I not only had a movie crew to lead and manage, I also had to do so for several weeks in an environment with real prisoners, some of whom were serving twenty-five years to life sentences for murder. We also cast local kids as extras and day players and brought in technical advisors—including Floyd Abrams, one of this country's greatest constitutional lawyers who's argued sixteen cases before the US Supreme Court. And we did so even though from my standpoint as a manager it would have been far easier to build the prison sets and hire professional actors to play the roles of the guards and the judge. We made these choices in part because they were cheaper and in part because, from a creative standpoint, the decision to use real locations and actual professional people lent an enormous amount of authenticity to the project. And we made a great effort to get that diversity and the authenticity that it offered.

In the prison scenes, for example, the real guards advised us that we should remove all jewelry, including Kate Beckinsale's wedding ring and earrings, and they taught me—because I stage and direct all the background—about color codes for prison uniforms. When I saw a hundred prisoners marching by twos, military style, in different-colored jumpsuits, the chief (assistant warden) explained that every prison is different but that one color would be standard issue, another is for "trustees" (prisoners with jobs, which diminishes time served by one-third), yet another for those who committed violent crimes like murder, another would signify sex offenders, and so on. That way, it's easy to identify dangerous individuals within the general population quickly. When we were filming a basketball game in the women's yard, we were advised that if one pant leg was rolled up, it was a gang symbol that the inmates would be punished for. Real prison guards and real cops know the protocol during a shakedown or when breaking up a fight. They know how to run a fingerprint machine, how the criminal would be treated, and which finger to print first. All this detail helped us stage our scenes and provide the film with contextual accuracy. *More diversity led us to greater creative quality.*

When we scout a prison, we go inside and observe. I look around and get a feel for the appearance (age, ethnicity, gender, physical condition, and so forth) of prisoners to help me better cast extras. We talk to wardens and guards. How are men's and women's prisons different? Who's allowed in a dormitory room? (Never a single guard alone.) What is protocol if there's a fight? (The guard waits outside the locked door until the riot team arrives.) Do the guards carry weapons? (Inside the cellblock, there are no guns, just batons.) How are the weapons carried, and when are they used? What is the demeanor of the prisoners? Hairstyles, tattoos, body language?

And we don't just do this when shooting in prisons. I've donned scrubs and witnessed eye surgery in an operating room at Lenox Hill Hospital in Manhattan so I could help better stage the eye-surgery scene in the Irwin Winkler film *At First Sight*. I've scouted the death chamber and spoken with the corrections officer at the Florida State Prison to learn how to stage the execution of Ed Harris's character in the film *Just Cause*. I've worked with actual members of New York City SWAT teams; homicide detectives; circus performers; farmers; shrimp fishermen; world-class opera singers; and the New York Giants, Yankees, and Knicks in order to learn the nuances of *their* jobs so I can better do *mine*. I am constantly observing humanity, protocol, demographics, stereotypes, and procedures. I rely on input from people from diverse walks of life, and I know that my ability to show them respect, to talk to them in their language and on their terms, allows me to smoothly integrate them into our workplace *and be a better manager so we get what we want—a better film.*

I can't treat a real prison guard like I might treat an actor—or a "normal" film set employee—they don't know our culture, union rules, or management norms any more than I know theirs. And because they have something we need to make the project inherently better, I have to show them a high level of professional respect—and just like it is with the rest of the crew, that respect is genuine.

So what can someone who admittedly works in an industry with a poor record of race and gender diversity tell you about how to manage diversity in your workplace? What specific strategies can be used to manage a diverse team when you need to maintain a high level of productivity, diminish tension, and maximize creativity? What are the techniques that can be adapted to *any* industry where the goal is to increase staff diversity—including race and gender—in order to maximize dollar efficiency and workplace cohesion while generating the highest level of creative output?

FIRST, VIEW THE DIVERSE KNOWLEDGE POOL AS
AN ASSET—REMEMBER, DIVERSITY INCREASES
PROFIT, STABILITY, AND INNOVATION—NOT AN
UNCOMFORTABLE "MANAGEMENT PROBLEM."

Embrace and welcome diversity of race, gender, background, and thought by hiring a diverse group of employees even though it may increase managerial challenges because it does two things—*it opens the minds of every member of your team to new ideas, and it sets a tone that facilitates creative problem-solving and, ultimately, greater success.*

NEXT, EMBRACE THE FACT THAT NOT EVERYONE
WILL THINK LIKE YOU DO, AND RECOGNIZE THAT
THAT'S A GOOD THING.

Acknowledge that people from different walks of life and different backgrounds, and those with different mind-sets, orientations, life experiences, and perspectives can be *managed best by downplaying the value of conformity and amping up respect for differences, alternative approaches, and novel ideas.*

THEN DEMOCRATIZE YOUR WORKPLACE AS WELL AS
YOUR MIND-SET.

Many workplaces accentuate hierarchies, not only with salaries and titles but also with larger offices, better furniture—even different lunchrooms. In many businesses, individual employees also take steps to separate themselves from "underlings," say, by wearing expensive clothes. Yet in filmmaking, where the salary and power levels are so radically different—an actor making millions of dollars will be performing ten feet from a union employee making $400 a day—the culture of the set has evolved to diminish those differences, which in turn facilitates a comfortable workplace environment. As different as we often are, we find our similarities. For the most part, we stand side by side in line to get food from the same caterer and then eat together at communal tables and suffer under the same workplace conditions. The "corporate uniform" of film production—regardless of salary or title—is blue jeans or shorts, a T-shirt, and sneakers—nothing that denotes income, job status, or power. When I was shooting *Just Cause* in Miami with director Arne Glimcher and Steven Spielberg dropped by the set to visit his wife, Kate Capshaw, who was the leading lady in the film, he wore blue jeans, sneakers, and a baseball hat just like the rest of us—including the production assistants. And since we work with people from all walks of life and all over the world, casual dress not only makes the cast and crew on set more uniform, but our casual dress is potentially less intimidating when we bring outsiders onto the set or travel to their places of work to shoot, as well. *In other words, democratizing the workplace not only helps build equity with the crew, as discussed in chapter 6, but it also serves to ease discomfort with atypical cast and crew members.*

WITH A DIVERSE TEAM, EXPECT ABNORMAL POWER SHIFTS AND ACCOMMODATE ACCORDINGLY.

When we were shooting a scene inside a school bus on *Nothing But the Truth*, in which Kate Beckinsale chaperones a school trip for her son's second-grade class, there was an extra—a little boy—sitting a few seats back from Kate who decided *after he was established in the scene* that he wanted to see his mother. We were shooting as the school bus was being driven on a highway outside of Memphis, and the little boy's mother was a couple of miles back at the staging area. I recognized immediately that a certain amount of power and control had just shifted to this seven-year-old. Yet I couldn't have someone take him to his mother and replace him because he had been established in the master shot we had already done for this scene. At the same time, I knew that if the situation wasn't remedied, we could lose the bulk of the day's work and/or the director would be forced to make some creative compromises. *The little boy needed to be managed*, and as a manager, I knew that *at that moment, he needed to be gently coerced and coddled*—not exactly in my job description, but it's something I occasionally have to do. So embrace the fact that with the *authenticity* and the *inspired creative solutions* that come with a diverse team, unusual management challenges will come, as well.

LEARN TO TOLERATE, NOT RIDICULE, THE
INCONSISTENCIES WE ALL EXHIBIT AS HUMAN
BEINGS, BECAUSE ON DIVERSE TEAMS THERE WILL
BE EVEN MORE OF THEM.

With a diverse group, there'll always be the vegetarian in a leather jacket at the catering table railing about someone eating meat. I once had an actress who insisted on an oxygen tank and mask because she couldn't tolerate the (nontoxic) FX smoke we were using on set—and I accommodated her. One of the crew took a photo of her holding the oxygen mask over her nose with one hand and a cigarette in the other. On *Glengarry Glen Ross*—a film with a preponderance of intense emotional scenes—Al Pacino, who played Ricky Roma, literally walked off the set during a take when he lost his concentration after someone on the crew rustled a sheet of paper. While waiting the ten minutes Al needed in his dressing room to get back into character, I reminded myself how important it is to exercise extreme diplomacy and to respect these personal differences—no one else walked off the set when the paper was rustled, but that hardly mattered. *Al* needed total concentration in order to get to the creative place he wanted and *we needed*. An overall attitude of broad acceptance of idiosyncrasies and differences—even those that may seem blatantly ridiculous to you—cultivates an atmosphere and sets a tone of acceptance, understanding, and tolerance that is helpful on diverse teams.

It is rather ironic, I think, that an industry operating under the extraordinary understanding of the value of diversity of skill set and professional perspective—an industry that reaps the benefits of that diversity through the authenticity it offers our final product—hinders itself by not having greater gender and race diversity at the highest decision-making, content-choosing, social commentary–making, culture-defining levels. Especially in light of the fact that race and gender parity in the film industry represents much more than "fairness" and access to good jobs. In the broadest sense, the current lack of equal representation of women and minorities represents a loss of creative perspective and valued voice. Every business should make it a goal to have a diverse management team and workforce not only because it's just and equitable but also to improve output, stability, and financial success. And for the businesses like film and television production and numerous others—like journalism, publishing, and advertising—where equal access to jobs also means equal access to contribute to the larger social conversation, we should work even harder to make sure that equity is achieved.

INSIGHT:

Optimizing and exploiting diversity is good for the bottom line.

Action Steps:

Strive to increase diversity of all types.

View diversity—race, gender, age, ethnicity, education, background, and the like—as an asset, not an uncomfortable "management problem."

Embrace the fact that not everyone will think like you do, and recognize that that's a good thing.

Democratize your workplace as well as your mind-set.

Expect abnormal power shifts and accommodate accordingly.

Learn to tolerate, not ridicule, inconsistencies.

Result:

A more diverse workforce that delivers greater innovation, superior problem-solving, higher profits, more stability, and greater overall success—and in industries that control content like film, more equitable access to voice, as well.

FIND THE HARD CORNERS

———————————★———————————

Then Build the Edges and Solve the Puzzle of
Decision-Making

Case Study:
The film *The Nutcracker*. Directed by Emile Ardolino; ballet
master in chief Peter Martins; starring the corps of the New
York City Ballet and Macaulay Culkin.

———————————————————————————————————————

Just as employers and employees benefit when vacation days
have anchors and limits, there is a plethora of data that suggests
that *unlimited* and *unbounded* don't work particularly well for a
lot of other things, either. When researchers studied levels of par-
ticipation in employer-offered 401(k)s, enrollment increased when
the investment options were limited to only a few. And when researchers set up a tasting-and-display table for flavors of a particular brand of jam in a California grocery store and offered shoppers
a coupon for purchase, the results provided some insight into just
how important limits can be—even in benign decision-making
situations. When presented with twenty-four flavor options and

the discount coupon, 3 percent of tasters proceeded to purchase the product. Yet when the tasting table had only six flavors, a full 30 percent of tasters proceeded to buy a jar. These results have been replicated over and over again with other products; we know that while we find the *concept* of more options appealing, in reality, *too many options can be overwhelming and often lead to either indecision or poor decisions.*

I first recognized this early in my career when I was tasked with scheduling films and realized that without clear limits to establish boundaries or "givens," the task of deciding what to do, when, and why was daunting for one very specific reason: without guiding parameters, the options and permutations were often just like those 401(k) investment options, that jam no one would buy, or those vacation days no one seems willing to take—*unlimited.*

As you can imagine, the process of scheduling a film is encumbered with a frighteningly long list of mitigating factors and competing priorities, and because there are so many variables and so many different ways to lay out a schedule, it can be difficult to figure out where to even *start.** On some of the early films I worked on, the task of scheduling a seventy-day shoot with, say, sixty actors, seventy-five locations, and two thousand extras could, at least initially, feel overwhelming. *Which scenes do we shoot on day one, and why? How about day forty-five and day sixty-three? And every other day?*

So I would start by looking for a rational reason *to begin*

---

* Remember, we don't shoot in sequential order from page one of the script, but rather create a financially sound production schedule that might include shooting scene seventeen, forty-five, and seventy-seven on one particular day because they are all in the same location.

somewhere or *do something first,* or *last,* or in a *particular sequence.* In other words, *I was looking for a rational way to limit my options.* I was looking for the biggest, most definitive, and nonnegotiable elements—noting perhaps that if we were doing a late-summer picture, all the exteriors would need to be shot before the leaves changed color so the scenes would match. Or that on this particular project, the leading man is only available until November 12. Or that we can only shoot at the heliport/restaurant/school during one specific week in September or only on Wednesdays after 6:00 P.M. I was looking for what I would come to call the *hard corners*—circumstances that limited my options when scheduling specific scenes. And as I got used to doing this, looking for those hard corners became my default process for virtually all the other decisions I had to make.

Once I began to anchor the process of scheduling a movie using the *hard-corner approach,* the process stopped feeling so daunting for this reason: *With those hard corners identified, I now had critical structure and immediate direction.* By isolating the primary immovable parts—*think of them as the four corners of a jigsaw puzzle*—followed by identifying the second tier of important decision-making restraints—*the straight edges of the scheduling puzzle*—I found that it became much easier to lay out the rest of the work. Identifying those hard corners and straight edges and making those initial scheduling decisions not only locked in dates and locations, but it also locked in the cast that worked at those locations—and any additional equipment and crew needed on those days, as well—which set into play a welcome cascade of direction-giving if-thens.

On *Devil's Advocate,* we were slated to shoot over a dozen

scenes at three different New York City courthouses. The court-houses were only available to us on weekends, and there was absolutely no flexibility. Instead of this "limit" being an encum-brance, from a scheduling standpoint, it was *liberating*. The courthouse scenes immediately emerged as hard corners that anchored our schedule for the entire film. Because we had to shoot the courthouse scenes on *weekends*, I now had to schedule two *weekdays* off for the cast and crew. And since we're only per-mitted by union rules to change the five days in our work week *once* on a film project (to protect the crew from working more than five days in a row due to exploitive scheduling practices), all the other elements incrementally began to fall into place—*simply because I established a single hard corner*. If that meant that an ac-tor would get paid on a run-of-the-picture deal instead of for, say, five weeks, I could live with it—and defend the decision (and the added expense) if I was challenged on it.

On *Sabrina*, when Sydney Pollack decided that he wanted to shoot all the scenes written for Paris *in Paris* rather than grabbing the establishing shots in France with a (smaller) second unit crew and "cheating" the bulk of the Paris scenes by shooting them in New York City (a commonly used and much cheaper alternative), that directorial creative mandate became a significant hard cor-ner that anchored the scheduling of the entire film.

The hard-corner approach also became instrumental as I scheduled *within each day* as well as *for the entire film*. For exam-ple, one day-to-day hard corner that makes my decision-making easier is to identify the department that will take the longest to set up for a particular shot. If we are doing a shot that uses a crane and that crane takes an hour and forty-five minutes to set up, that's my hard corner. That means that I can allow makeup and hair the hour and ten minutes they asked for without any further thought. I don't care about the thirty minutes electric needs to set up the three Ten-Ks (big lights), so I'm not pushing them or cracking the whip because they'll be ready long before the grips have the crane up. It's a yes to the leading man who wants to get his hair trimmed, and the child actors can be sent to tutoring, as well. Once I've identified that the hard corner is the hour and forty-five minutes needed to set up the crane, everything else falls into place.

By implementing the hard-corner approach as if it were a string of managerial code, I could tackle all sorts of amorphous and overwhelming tasks, as well as make decisions with greater speed and efficiency because *identifying the hard corners provides direction and structure in such a way that it eliminates a lot of potential options.* Because all my decisions are grounded in sound, rational thought, they are correct more often, and I feel far more confident in them—which is important since they're often tough calls, and I may need to justify them.

All these management strategies I am putting forth in this book are intertwined and self-supporting. And everyone's hard corners in their own business will be different. But once you know to look for hard corners, they are usually pretty easy to identify.

The hard-corner approach effectively allows us to use *choice architecture* to our advantage by limiting options in situations where the choices are normally overwhelmingly *unlimited*.

Hard corners can be *big* or they can be small.

One of the first *big* hard corners that I identified, and one that I use to process every decision I make while shooting a film, is that *we have to make a day's work no matter what.* The reason for this is that we are scheduled and budgeted for *an exact number of days,* and we pay for each and every one of those days *whether we get usable footage or not.* Bracketed by that single hard corner—*which choice drives us toward that goal with more certainty?*—most of my decisions are far easier to make. Oddly, as simplistic—and perhaps as obvious—as this filmmaking mandate may appear to be, I can't tell you how many well-known directors and producers will ignore, or forget, that overriding hard corner—*get a day's work no matter what*—again and again.

But let's say you run a small business and you decide that your hard corner is "the customer is always right." Once that is articulated, all decisions become easier to make. Or say you are contracted to pave a section of highway and you note that ramp seven has to be handled differently during paving because it provides access to a hospital—that becomes a significant hard corner. Or let's say that you are planning a vacation and decide the hard corner is that the kids have a good time—that will likely simplify a lot of the decisions you need to make by taking them in a specific direction.

But let's apply the hard-corner approach to a far more serious situation. Say you are a parent with a sick child and you are given two radically different medical opinions from two equally qualified and respected surgeons. The first surgeon tells you the child has a "hot" appendix and needs to be operated on immediately or he may die. The second surgeon tells you that it's *not* appendicitis, and the best course of action is to wait and see (this was a common dilemma before antibiotic treatment became a viable third option for the treatment of appendicitis in 2015). As the parent of that child, you are facing two equally qualified yet dramatically conflicting opinions, and you are looking for one thing only: *definitive direction.*

What you need is a hard corner. So you ask yourself, *What is the single most important thing to me at this moment?* That answer is simple: that your child survives.

The doctors both told you that an appendectomy is a safe and easy operation with little associated risk. With that stated, and against the backdrop of your now articulated hard corner, the decision just got really easy to make—and easy to rationalize. You recognize that the risk of *not doing the operation* is much greater than the risk of *doing the operation.* With the hard corner of survival articulated and in place, you can now not only *make* the decision to go with the doctor who wants to operate but you can also feel justified in that decision *regardless of whether or not once in surgery the doctor determines that he was wrong and the appendix really didn't need to come out.*

By framing the inherent risk in those two options around a reasonable hard corner, you effectively made a hard emotional decision much easier to make, in part because that hard corner gave you direction by limiting options—*the decision to not operate no longer looked like a good choice*—but also in part because identifying that hard corner allowed you to convert what could have been a "hot" emotional decision into a "cold" rational one.

A hot decision is one made in a stress- and emotion-fueled situation, and it is less likely to be correct than a cold or rationally thought-out decision. And hot emotional decisions aren't reserved for medical crises about family members; they populate many workplace circumstances, as well. On set, shooting a film, I am in an environment that mandates taking what could be high-stress, rapid-fire, think-and-respond decisions that will have big financial and artistic consequences and making them in a low-stress, rational way. Identifying hard corners assists me in putting a system in place to translate what could be hot, emotional decisions into cold, rational ones.

Behavioral researchers explain that the people who can do that the best are people who do it all the time—people involved in stressful jobs or who participate in extreme sports like big-wave surfing or wingsuit flying—people who are forced to make life-and-death decisions over and over again in fast-moving, high-risk situations. The process of repeatedly doing this is what equips police officers, trauma surgeons in the ER, or—because of practice on simulators—a commercial airline pilot like Chesley B. "Sully" Sullenberger III to make life-and-death decisions like those involved in landing a jetliner with two failed engines in the Hudson River in what appears to be a state of unnatural calm. These individuals have been trained to convert those hot emotional moments into cold, calculated, rational decision events— something pilots call *deliberate calm*.

Whenever I think of hot-and-cold decision-making, I remember the scene from the film *Six Days Seven Nights* where Robin Monroe (played by Anne Heche) asks Quinn Harris (played by Harrison Ford) how he managed to stay so calm while he crash-landed his airplane on an uninhabited island during an electrical storm when the two were en route to Tahiti. He responds by saying, "I'm the captain. That's my job. It's no good for me to go waving my arms in the air screaming, 'Oh shit, we're going to die.'" His character's training as a pilot directed him to calm, rational, cold decision-making—*deliberate calm*—in what was a hot, emotional situation. That was the same skill that likely helped guide Harrison—who is an avid pilot in real life—when he really did crash-land a plane at Penmar Golf Course in Southern California years later. In both cases—one fictional and one real—Harrison Ford's hard corner was just like that of the parent with the sick child: *survive*. And that in turn directed him to *deliberate calm*.

Doctors in the ER are given a hard corner by Hippocrates: *first, to do no harm*, and they—along with first responders, triage nurses, and other emergency workers—are also given other hard corners in the form of mandated procedure—if a patient presents with *X*, he or she must immediately be given *Y*. *Reflect for a moment on how welcome these hard corners must be and how they simplify and direct the decisions of a doctor or medical professional by converting what could be hot, emotional decisions into cold, rational ones.* By combining the benefits of practice-induced *deliberate calm* with the direction provided by a relevant, overriding hard corner, these high-pressure decision-makers will be in a better position to make rational, thought-out decisions that produce better outcomes.

Researchers have found that anyone involved in day-in-and-day-out hot decision-making will get better at converting those hot, emotional moments to cold, rational decisions through *practice*. Pilots get that practice in flight simulators, first responders go through simulations and training exercises, and researchers also report that playing action video games, specifically "shooter games," have a similar effect. In fact, any activity that requires making consecutive *big*-impact decisions under duress where you can't take your time or form a committee or sleep on it—whether that's in a high-stress job like firefighting, a high-risk action sport, a high-performance organization, or a shooter video game—requires repeatedly translating those hot, emotional moments into cold, rational ones. What I've found is that in addition to *practice*, overlaying a structure offered by identifying the hard corners helps this process enormously. Because decisions based on hard corners are based on a sound, logical foundation, they don't get stalled in emotion and fear or in a quagmire of indecisiveness, corporate power struggles, or committee-style decision vetting.

But there is something else going on here, as well.

A hard corner also gets you where you want to go *faster*. And that is not a small thing.

John Boyd, the military strategist and United States Air Force colonel who developed the now widely used OODA decision loop (Observe, Orient, Decide, Act), deduced that historically the armies that won the toughest battles didn't necessarily have the best equipment, and they weren't necessarily the biggest in terms of manpower. Instead, the winning military units had *superior decision-making abilities*. Boyd concluded that the armies with personnel who could *observe, orient, decide,* and *act* the fastest (in other words, progress through the OODA loops the fastest) won more battles. He concluded that agility—*a combination of "speed in decision-making" and "cohesiveness of units"*—was the defining factor in military success. The faster you could *observe* and *orient*, the sooner you got to *decide* and *act*. Which in turn brought you to the next situation—separated perhaps only by fractions of a second from the last—where you again would need to *observe* and *orient* and then *decide* and *act*.

What I have found in my filmmaking experience is that in effect, using hard corners as a framework aids a decision-maker in accelerating that loop of successive, refined decisions that lead to success by providing a rubric that isolates what Boyd called "the main focus of the effort." What hard corners do is facilitate speedy and agile decision-making and pave the way for incremental improvements. When discussing long-term business survival—something completely irrelevant to what we do in film production because our life cycle is so short (remember the fruit fly analogy?)—Rita Gunther McGrath, a professor of management at the Columbia Business School, concludes that for companies looking to compete, "fast and roughly right decision making will replace deliberations that are precise but slow."

And there are other factors that come into play.

ONCE THE HARD CORNERS ARE IDENTIFIED, THE DECISION-MAKER HAS TO HAVE THE AUTHORITY TO ACT.

One thing that I've been hammering home is that because of the high cost of production, the number of unions and their rules, and the difficult-to-control, out-in-the-elements nature of filmmaking, we operate under a tight schedule and tight constraints. Because of that, in order to succeed, we have to function as a *high-performance organization*. What that means is that we place a high value on *both* the *speed* and the *quality* of our day-to-day performance. And that means that in addition to the decision-maker needing to be able to convert what could be *hot decisions* into *cold decisions* on a regular basis and make fast and high-quality critical operating decisions, that decision-maker has to have the *authority to act*. That requires there to be, along with *decisiveness* on the part of the decision-maker, *authority* from above and *respect* among the rank and file for that authority.

RECOGNIZE THAT OFTEN, *A* DECISION IS BETTER
THAN *NO* DECISION.

What I have argued thus far is that the beauty of underpinning decisions with hard corners is first that they provide much-needed direction, and second that they streamline the process of identifying your end goal in a manner that gets you to a *correct* decision *faster*. But there is another part to this equation. In decision-making, we often *don't* have perfect information or the ability to predict all outcomes through rational thought. There are many situations—and not just in filmmaking—where there isn't necessarily a predictable *correct decision*. There is just *a* decision. It is important for decision-makers to recognize the situations where *a decision* is better than *no decision* and acknowledge that fact. Doing so empowers the decision-maker to act without hesitation.

In the case of filmmaking, because time is literally money to the tune of $20,000 an hour and our hard corner is to *make a day's work no matter what*, in some cases making *a decision* drives us toward that goal regardless (within reason) of *what* that decision is. In other words, often *a decision* is better than *no decision* or indecisiveness for one simple reason—it moves us forward in our day. And since every day is so expensive, in situations where there is no clear "right" decision, the worst-case scenario would be *indecisiveness*. I sometimes make calls that could go either way and do so with confidence knowing that the sooner I *decide* and *act*, the sooner the crew is working toward the goal of *making a day's work, no matter what*.

The instant that I make a decision—for example, that we're

going to a cover set,[†] or buying a meal penalty—it means an *idle* crew is now a *working* crew moving closer to the finish line, which is defined for us as getting two and a half pages of the script in the can by the day's wrap. Indecisiveness in times when there is often no "right decision" but rather there is just a need for a definitive call and forward motion is counterproductive and expensive. Say we're scheduled to shoot exteriors and there's more than a 30 percent chance of rain. I'll make the call to move to a cover set without thinking about it twice because we simply can't afford the risk of being rained out. And because that decision is based on such a sound premise—a hard corner—just like the parent of the sick child, I don't second-guess the decision even, in this example, if it *doesn't* rain that day.

MAKE SURE THAT THE HARD CORNERS ARE IDENTIFIED BY A KEYSTONE MANAGER.

Sydney Finkelstein, a professor at Dartmouth's Tuck School of Business, isolates situations where the decision-maker has self-interest in the outcomes as one of the Achilles' heels of good decision-making. In my position as a keystone manager, I essentially have no self-interest since my job is structured so that my goal is *the success of the project as a whole,* as I oversee different departments and individuals that very often have siloed agendas.

The financial crisis of 2008 is perhaps the most compelling example of a hard corner that was miscued because of self-serving agendas. Minus governing regulations and keystone managers with

[†] A *cover set* is a backup set we can film on if we have problems with weather, cast availability, or other issues.

objective eyes on the big picture, operating under the hard corner that we want a stable, prosperous, global economy, many involved—banks, mortgage brokers, those involved with mortgage-backed securities at investment banks (and even a few borrowers)—worked under the hard corner that served *them; make as much money as possible no matter what.* In some cases, that hard corner was underpinned by outright greed—even criminal behavior. In other cases, it was a result of a profound miscalculation; the belief that real estate values would continue to grow at irrational rates and outpace accelerating interest rates. *What this tells us is that hard corners can be driven by both faulty assumptions and misguided, self-serving, personally skewed agendas.* Conversely, if identified correctly and used as a filter in decision-making, hard corners can be significant drivers of success. But for them to fuel better outcomes, they have to be overseen by either a keystone manager functioning without a skewed personal agenda or by regulations that legislate with eyes on the whole game, not self-serving, shortsighted, siloed short wins.

Sometimes the hard corners are easy to identify.

When Ashley Judd's character, Jane, in *Someone Like You* had a fantasy about cows dressed in hula skirts in a bridal shop window in Manhattan, it meant that we had to actually dress cows in hula skirts and get them to stand in a real storefront window in Soho. The fact that cows don't like to ride in elevators, don't climb stairs, and really don't take direction very well became a very significant set of hard corners that day, and we based a lot of decisions on those facts. Everything centered on what the cows would, or would not, do.

But it's worth noting that as easy as some hard corners like this one are to identify, others are not so obvious. And this should give all managers pause.

BECAUSE SOMETIMES WE CAN MISS THE HARD CORNERS ALTOGETHER.

One hard corner that *I missed completely* occurred when we were about to begin filming a movie version of George Balanchine's *The Nutcracker*. And the hard corner that I missed had to do with Darci Kistler's legs. Well, not just *her* legs, but also the legs of the entire corps of the New York City Ballet.

I had spent decades working with world-class actors—Al Pacino, Sir John Gielgud, John Huston, Barbra Streisand, Jack Lemmon, Tom Hanks—where we routinely did ten to fifteen takes on a single camera setup. Indeed, the director Stanley Kubrick was famous for doing fifty takes or more *on almost everything*. The critical, game-changing hard corner that I missed on *The Nutcracker* was that *dancers have only four or five takes in their legs*. After that, muscle fatigue sets in, and their elevations aren't perfect, and that reality applied to Darci as well as the other fifty or so dancers in the film.

In my defense, I had never filmed a ballet before, and the single largest hard corner that should have framed the entire project—the fact that we couldn't get more than a few takes out of the dancers' legs—never occurred to me. *And it never occurred to anyone else to tell me.* As a result, the original schedule I had done for the film completely fell apart. When I finally figured out that the dancers couldn't do take five, let alone take fourteen . . .

or fifty-two—especially if there were challenging leaps, toe work, or elevations—I now had to reschedule a good portion of the project around this new anchoring piece of information. So I sat down with the director and ballet master and determined which dances were the most challenging. I then shifted the work around to pair less demanding scenes—for instance, the Christmas Eve party in the first act is relatively easy, but "Coffee" and "Tea" require difficult elevations by the principal dancers. Armed with this new information, I was able to reschedule the material appropriately.

Once the fact that the dancers' legs could only sustain a handful of takes became our overriding hard corner, we had to completely alter our approach to filming as well as our schedule. Rather than shooting with a single camera, we used multiple cameras simultaneously (generally five), which meant carrying additional equipment and extra camera crews. There was also added pressure to get a perfect performance on *both sides of the camera*. If a dancer made a misstep, *or* if a camera assistant blew focus, or any one of a hundred other technical flaws occurred that would be of less concern on a normal film shoot, the consequences would have a far greater impact.

What I've learned is that a manager basing decisions on hard corners increases the tensile strength of his or her organization not only because those decisions are *far more likely to be the right choices*, will be *arrived at with greater speed*, and *will be delivered with more conviction*, but also because those decisions *are so factually grounded they make logical sense to everyone involved and therefore build trust in leadership*. And over time, that fact works to increase a manager's confidence in himself or herself and to increase the confidence the team has in that manager, as well, which improves efficiency across the board.

INSIGHT:

Too many options are counterproductive. Identifying the hard corners that frame a decision is a simple and constructive way to set parameters and limit options in decision-making.

Action Steps:

Take the time to isolate the hard corners in any decision-making situation.

Incorporate those hard corners into your forward-moving strategy.

Recognize that there are situations when there is no single "right" decision and that in those cases *a* decision is often better than *no* decision as it moves you forward.

Result:

A streamlined, expedited decision-making process that creates less stress, more confidence, and better outcomes.

9

ADOPT A CRISIS-MANAGEMENT MODEL

———————————★*———————————*

AND CREATE YOUR OWN RICHTER SCALE

CASE STUDY:
The film *The Purple Rose of Cairo*. Orion. Directed by Woody
Allen; starring Jeff Daniels, Mia Farrow, and Dianne Wiest.

EVERY DAY WE'RE shooting, I face a seemingly never-ending on-
slaught of questions and problems from the crew—*Are we filming
the interior of the 747 at the airport in Newark or in Orlando? When
can I mic the actors? How many bullet hits do we need in the wall?
Are we shooting the apartment in Paris or building it in New York?
How many people are we bringing to the amphitheater in Sicily? What
time is the call tomorrow? How many bridesmaids for the wedding
scene? Where do you want us to put the tiger?**

---

* In *The Prince of Tides*, directed by Barbra Streisand, Tom Wingo's father keeps
a tiger caged outside of the gas station he owns. When we were shooting, the
tiger was kept in a circus cage that had to be wheeled into position and set to
camera.

Then there's the constant barrage of snafus, complications, and last-minute developments—*The generator's down. The Gulf-stream jet we booked for tomorrow is delayed due to weather in Abu Dhabi. The lead actress announces—just as we're preparing to shoot her water scenes—that she can't swim. It's 4:00 A.M., and the antique car we are using in the shot has a dead battery. The herd of cows we're filming won't take direction . . .*

In fact, there are so many questions and problems when making a movie that it's not uncommon for a line to form on set as crew members wait for the chance just to *ask me something*. Of course, because we do so much exhaustive and painstakingly detailed planning in preproduction, most of these questions are easy to answer right off the top of my head or after a quick glance at my strip board or shooting schedule. But some require on-the-fly decisions that are not so easy—decisions that often have to be made as we shoot on location, out in the elements, at all hours of the day and night. This is a rapid-fire *ask-decide-respond-commit* environment where there's no time to take things "under advisement." And to make matters even more difficult, these are often decisions that will have a big financial impact and numerous flow-through consequences.

Early in my career, it was a challenge to not fall victim to spending all day, every day, steeped in stress, feeling—and responding—like I was straddling a workplace San Andreas Fault, where everything I was presented with appeared to be a crisis of earth-shattering, quake-like proportions. As I moved up through the ranks and gained responsibility, it became clear that if I wanted to survive—let alone excel—I had to learn how to modulate my reactions and defuse what could have become an unacceptable level of productivity-, efficiency-, and sanity-busting pressure.

To help me deal with the daily assault of the not-so-easy-to-address problems and questions, I first had to change my meta-perspective from one where I *resented* questions and problems to one where I *expected* them—after all, that was part of my job. Then I had to recognize and acknowledge that all these questions and problems *weren't* actually crises—even though admittedly, in the moment, they often felt as if they were.

In order to accomplish this, I found it enormously helpful to establish a simple scale for "grading" problems—a scale similar to what the Richter and moment management scales do for earthquakes, or what triage nurses do for patients in hospital emergency rooms.

Basically, I began assessing everything on a scale of 1–10, and any issue that I assigned a 5 or below, I classified as within the realm of normal. Anything given a 6 or 7 was considered borderline, and anything classified at an 8 or above I considered a crisis.

Once I began using this strategy, it helped to reinforce the fact that most things *weren't a crisis*. And by reframing in my head the fact that the vast majority of the issues I was being presented with were actually par for the course and completely normal, it allowed me to handle everything with a higher success rate and less stress. Which is not to say that I did *nothing* for those problems *not* considered a crisis—they were still real issues that needed *careful thought* and *specific action, as well.*

Referring back to some of the examples I mentioned earlier: Say it was 6:00 A.M. and I just arrived on set and was told that the generator for the makeup trailer had broken down. *As much as I would have viewed this as a crisis early in my career, with my scale in place, I classify it as only a 2.* That Gulfstream jet flying in from Abu Dhabi that we'd scheduled to use in a scene in New York the following day that had been delayed due to weather? That, too, would have been a crisis in my mind when I was starting out, but with my numeric problem-grading system in place, *I realize that it's maybe a 3*, and I remind myself of that before I react. That night in the woods when the battery died in the 1949 Packard at 4:00 A.M. and the car wouldn't start? A non-filmmaker might view that as less of a problem than the broken generator or the delayed jet, but it's actually bigger. *For me, that was teetering on a 5.* But I reminded myself that a 5 is not an 8 and that it's not a big enough problem to command an adrenaline firestorm or extreme measures.

THIS SCALE ISN'T ARBITRARY.

The reason that the events listed above weren't 8s or higher—or full-blown crises—is that I'd determined that they were all *solvable problems with the resources that we had on hand, and they wouldn't cripple us in a way we couldn't recover from.* For me, that's the salient metric that delineates a crisis from a normal problem. So the first question I ask myself when I am presented with a problem is always, *Can this issue be solved with the assets we have on hand, and is the damage containable?*

Here's how those specific numerical classifications were arrived at:

At 6:00 A.M., I already have one electrician on location who can hot-wire the out-of-commission generator (a not uncommon occurrence on films). It gets a grade of 2 because, while it will cost the makeup department some time, I'm confident that we can make that time up. I know the actors aren't needed on set for several hours, so we're good.

In the case of the weather-delayed G-5 (which happened to us on the Sydney Pollack / Harrison Ford film *Sabrina*), I immediately scheduled a move to a cover set for the next shooting day where we could accomplish a day's work. That got assigned a 3 because, while it was inconvenient, with the hard corner of *get a day's work done no matter what* covered, it was hardly a crisis. We wouldn't lose any time or money by flipping one full day of work for another, so I made the call setting everything in motion and moved on.

In the case of the Packard that wouldn't start at 4:00 A.M. (this occurred in the woods in Rhode Island when we were filming *Evening*, and not only was the battery in the car dead but the backup battery was dead, too), that was a bigger problem—a 5—*because it happened when we were actually shooting that scene—which meant that we had zero time to get in front of the problem.* There was no way to get a new battery or a different car out in the woods at that hour—or to substitute any other work—and time was of the essence since we were shooting a night scene, and we only had another hour of darkness left. So we made the *financial* decision to make an *artistic* compromise. Instead of the car being driven by the actor as planned, we had the props put the car into neutral and push it into frame as the actor sat behind the wheel pretending to drive. The shot was changed creatively to accommodate this, and while it wasn't exactly what the director wanted or what we had planned, it saved the night, and we made our work.

With this numeric classification scale in place, I handle the 5s and below—or normal problems—to the best of my ability and then, very intentionally and systematically, dismiss them, along with any associated stress. I do this knowing that every single one of these decisions was made easier because it was numerically graded, determined to be solvable in a way that didn't cost us much time or money, and was predicated by my hard corner—to *make a day's work no matter what.* Every one of the problems discussed above was solved while still doing that.

Once I began assessing the magnitude of problems in such a calculated and deliberate way, the impact it had in terms of improving productivity and dollar efficiency proved to be *highly functional*, and, interestingly, those benefits were *highly contagious,* as well. When I didn't react to everything with stress, it didn't just make me feel better—it built the confidence the crew had in me and improved morale and the work environment, and that increased the tensile strength of the crew on a very human level.

If I'm calm and acting with certitude, it diminishes the crew's stress—as well as mine—and those crew members can then go back to *their* teams with elevated calm and confidence, too. Also—and this is important—just like hard corners do, that calm, decisive demeanor expedites the problem-solving time frame. Overreacting, vacillating, and being indecisive rarely leads to productive solutions or gets you where you want to go in a time-efficient manner.

As simple as this advice appears to be, it's significant for a number of reasons. For starters, no one in a high-stress job can function effectively in a nonstop state of what is called *acute stress response* (fight or flight). And while there is research that suggests that in certain situations stress may *improve* functionality, for most of us, constant high stress *diminishes* our performance and *lowers* workplace engagement. Researchers have found that under extremely high stress our cognitive ability often declines and we process details poorly. We lose visual and auditory acuity as we develop tunnel vision and auditory exclusion—meaning that under stress, we're prone to miss important details.

Even though the stress I feel and the magnitude of what is at stake in my job as a filmmaker isn't remotely on the level of what is often faced by doctors, military personnel, law enforcement, emergency workers, airline pilots, and others, I've found it extremely helpful to intentionally teach myself to employ *deliberate calm*, and using the 1–10 numeric scale helps me do that.

But I also had to learn that if I deemed something to be an 8 or above, *I had to go into all-out crisis mode.* And that required me to have a whole other plan in place.

An issue designated an 8 or higher requires first *acknowledging that it is in fact a crisis*, followed by *understanding that to be remedied it will warrant greater effort than a normal problem*, and then accepting that it will *generate a higher level of stress*.

For those 8s and higher, I first identify the hard corner(s).

As helpful as hard corners are in improving outcomes in the management of normal, everyday events by providing definitive direction, limiting options, and accelerating the decision-making timeline, those hard corners are even more valuable when dealing with a crisis—even a crisis of extreme magnitude.

Raymond McPartland, a lead instructor and curriculum development specialist in the NYPD's Counterterrorism Division's Training Section involved in retraining the thirty-five thousand officers of the New York City Police Department to deal with active shooter cases in 2015, was doing so specifically because the hard corner that needed to be employed in these cases had changed. Citing the horrific Columbine High School shooting in Littleton, Colorado, in 1999; the terrorist attack in Mumbai, India, where ten Pakistani men connected to the terror group Lashkar-e-Tayyiba executed coordinated attacks in multiple locations, murdering 164 people over four days in November 2008; and the terror attacks at multiple locations in Paris, France, in November 2015 that took the lives of 130 people; New York Police Commissioner Bill Bratton reported that hostage taking in many active shooter cases is no longer a means to an end that involves the hostage takers negotiating to *get something* as the case had so often been in the past. The "hostages" in many of the recent active shooter cases were not being held as assets for negotiation but instead were being used as decoys and "distractions" that afforded the shooters additional time to extend the duration of the killing spree and murder more victims.

Because of this fundamental shift from *hostage as leverage in negotiating* to *hostage as decoy*, the hard corner the police used in these cases had to change. What had previously been an approach guided by the premise that *we should go slowly and wait to see what the hostage takers want so we can end this peacefully* became *get in fast and neutralize the shooters before they kill even more people.* That shift required police officers and counterterrorism teams to understand that the faster they got to the shooters, the more lives they would save. The hard corner went from *approach with caution* to *move with lightning speed.*

McPartland explained that he was involved in retraining the entire NYPD to proceed in active shooter cases with a newly assigned, single-focused mission to disable the gunmen, and do it fast. He reported that the focused mission to *get in fast and get the shooters* represents more than a shift in the speed of the initial response. Working under that hard corner—although he didn't frame it using that specific term—also requires retraining officers to operate *counter to their instincts* once they've breached the crime scene perimeter. The *shooters fast and shooters first* mandate means ignoring previous protocol that had officers get victims out and check bags or backpacks (that might contain explosives) before they reached the killers. Now, instead, the NYPD is being trained—as difficult as this is to do—to initially ignore wounded victims and suspicious packages and proceed with laser focus to neutralize the shooters. One of the key benefits of a well-defined hard corner like *make a day's work no matter what,* or in this example, *shooters fast and shooters first,* is that its clearly delineated, fact-based structure not only produces better outcomes in an accelerated time frame—in active shooter cases, it actually saves lives—but it also creates a comforting sense for those involved that *they know exactly what they are doing and why they are doing it.* A hard corner provides *reasoned direction* and *rational justification* for a particular procedure. And while that proves to be highly valuable in everyday decision-making, it is even more valuable in a crisis.

BEYOND THE HARD CORNER(S).

In my experience, facing an 8, 9, or 10 means acknowledging that I am in crisis mode, identifying the hard corner(s), and then, very systematically, taking three, very specific additional steps.

First, objectify the problem. Next, contain the damage. And then purposefully act.[†]

I use these three sequential steps—*objectify, contain, act*—very successfully as my crisis-management rubric, sometimes even for the borderline problems that are graded 6s and 7s, or just short of a crisis.

Here's how it works:

Take the uncooperative cows I mentioned earlier that we encountered when we were shooting on a dairy farm in Hunterdon County while filming the opening scene for *Someone Like You*. As the film opens, Ashley Judd is explaining in voiceover what she calls the "new cow theory" of male mating behavior as we see a series of shots of cows standing around covered in flies, exiting a barn, and chewing their cud. For this sequence, the director, Tony Goldwyn, also wanted to get a shot of the herd of cows all looking in the same direction—in this case, camera right. Now, you can easily ask a group of actors—even child actors—to all look in a certain direction, but cows are a different story; they're not inclined to follow direction. And nothing we tried to coax them to "look over here" that day was working.

[†] This is an iteration of Boyd's OODA Loop mentioned in chapter 8. The key difference is that my rubric calls for problems to be *contained*, which is an important step in many business crises.

We got all the shots we needed for this opening sequence by the wrap on a Friday—except for the one of the cows looking camera right. Since Tony wanted this shot, the studio agreed to let us return the next day to get it even though it would be a premium day—Saturday—with the crew in double time. The problem was that we couldn't get the cows to do what we wanted, and the crew clock was ticking.

I declared this *almost an 8*, and because the hard corner that drives my decisions—*make a day's work no matter what*—was at risk, I applied my crisis-management rubric even though this fell just short of a crisis. Because we were in double time, it meant this day cost us two days of pay for everyone on the crew, and it looked like we weren't going to accomplish even *one day's work*.

So I *objectified* the problem. The director *wanted* this particular shot but didn't really *need* it to make the film work—which isn't always the case. Acknowledging that this shot fell into the category of *nice but not necessary* objectified the problem for me in a forward-moving, decision-making, stress-reducing manner.

Next, I *contained* the damage. In the afternoon when it was looking like we weren't going to get the shot, we put a call in to the studio to see what our budget restraints were if we didn't, and they told us what we expected to hear—they wouldn't authorize another shooting day or any additional overtime to get it. I now had a new hard corner because this "cow problem" was now contained to a single day. *We would either get this shot or we wouldn't.* That fact contained both *the financial loss* and *the creative mandate*.

Then I *acted*. Working within the allotted time frame, the farmhands and props kept gathering up the cows when they wandered off, and we kept trying to get them to all face in the same direction in unison, and we kept filming, eventually getting some usable—but not optimum—footage. And then we wrapped.

BUT WHAT HAPPENS WHEN PROBLEMS GET INCREMENTALLY BIGGER?

The actress who couldn't swim was Brittany Murphy on the film *Uptown Girls*, and we were slated to shoot a scene where she had to jump off of a small bridge in Central Park into what is called "the Lake." The problem was she had neglected to tell anyone that she was afraid of the water and didn't know how to swim—that is, until we were standing on the Bow Bridge overlooking the water with a full crew. I classified this as a $100,000, hard-corner-busting 8.5; a baffling *"You read the script. You know what we are shooting today. How did the fact that you can't swim not come up until now?"* kind of problem. We had about fifty extras, our requisite several tons of equipment and a hundred-person crew assembled in Central Park, and very little we could shoot. *And this was a shot that we actually needed for the film.*

So again, I *objectified* the problem and immediately deduced that we could salvage *half* the day. Then I *contained* the damage by making the decision to shoot what we could and punt the rest of the material to a future date. And then I *acted*. We shot Brittany's material with her standing on top of the bridge and got the shots with the stunt double—as scheduled—for the actual jump into the water. We then wrapped early and added a shooting day later in the schedule to get the Brittany-in-the-water shots at a lake on Staten Island, and on that day we actively prepared for our nonswimmer. We made numerous accommodations, including bringing in a platform for her to jump off and putting two scuba divers in the water to hold her up. Expensive and time-consuming, but the problem was contained to less than a day's loss, and we were able to complete a scene that was central to the movie.

By combining the 1–10 rating system with the rubric to *objectify, contain,* and *act,* I am much more able to stabilize situations in a very productive, forward-moving manner. Not only does it reduce stress but it also provides logical direction for fast and efficient resolution of each particular problem.

But so far, I've discussed this methodology regarding problems that, at best, have only hovered around an 8. How does this numerical grading system and problem-solving rubric to *objectify, contain,* and *act* work in a bona fide crisis?

Say, an as-bad-as-it-gets 10?

AFTER THREE MONTHS of prep, and after day five of shooting the Woody Allen film *The Purple Rose of Cairo*, I got a phone call at home from the producer Bobby Greenhut informing me that Woody had just told him that he wanted to replace the leading man (Michael Keaton). Now, depending on the specific circumstances, deciding to replace a lead actor *after* we've commenced principal photography can be a minor hiccup or about as big a crisis as you can face in the film business.

The fact is, Woody has replaced cast members for creative differences on a number of pictures, and it's rarely a big problem. For example, on *September,* he originally cast Sam Shepard in the role of Lane's (Mia Farrow) neighbor Peter. A few days into shooting, Sam was replaced with Christopher Walken—again due to creative differences. Then, after several more days of filming with Chris, the character of Peter was again recast, this time with the role going to Sam Waterston.[‡] But unlike what we would face on *Purple Rose*, the recasting issue on *September* wasn't a crisis because that particular film was contained to shooting in one house that was built on a soundstage. That meant that we could shoot any scene without Peter—and there were plenty of them—on virtually any day with only minimal complications as Woody worked to find a replacement. Therefore, we had no cast, location, or scheduling issues of any real significance.

But *Purple Rose* presented a different type of problem altogether.

For starters, in this case, as for a stopgap effort, we had a limited amount we *could* shoot. Obviously, we couldn't film any scenes the leading man was in because *we didn't have one*. But on *Purple Rose*, unlike *September*, being able to shoot any scenes this particular character wasn't in was tricky. Because Keaton's character was the lead—in fact, he played two parts, Tom Baxter and Gil Shepherd—he was in most of the scenes. On top of that, we were shooting this film on numerous live locations—not on a built set on a soundstage—and because it was a period film set in the 1920s, everything in frame had to be authentic to the time period. That meant every single detail needed to be planned for and scheduled *well in advance*. Every actor and extra in a scene (in the film we had upward of two thousand of them) would need period

---

[‡] After we shot the entire film with Sam Waterston playing the role of Peter, Woody kept Sam but recast several other roles, and we actually reshot the entire film from the beginning.

costumes (designed and fitted for the principal actors), period makeup, period hairstyles, and period props (eyeglasses, watches, briefcases, grocery carts, etc.). Every set, every street, and every automobile had to be authentic to the 1920s, as well—and in this case, at this early stage in the shooting schedule, most of those sets weren't slated to be ready for *weeks if not months*. Just to give you a single example, for our exteriors we had to remove any aluminum siding, air conditioners, TV antennas, and traffic lights for several blocks in all directions ahead of time in preparation for filming. That required making deals with local authorities, businesses, and homeowners. We needed to create and erect three-story building façades to put in front of any contemporary structures—such as a gas station that had modern pumps and architecture. Indeed, we had made a deal with the town of Piermont, New York, to sporadically take over the entire main street over the course of six weeks so we could convert it back in time to the 1920s. *And we had planned all this according to a preset schedule that was now, to a large degree, out the window.*

In any crisis like this, the option is to either *cut* losses and abandon the project or *stem* losses, turn things around, and reframe and salvage the project. With Michael Keaton now out, those were the two options available to us. Shut down and abandon the project, or salvage the film, recast the leading man, and then systematically piece together a new and viable schedule—which would include reshooting those first five days.[§]

[§] Temporarily shutting down or going into hiatus wasn't practical since that would have been prohibitively expensive. Furthermore, there is no insurance to cover an issue like this. If, for example, we had to shut down because an actor

If we canceled the project, all the money and effort spent during the months of preproduction—on scheduling, budgeting, scouting locations, set construction, cast and crew salaries, and rental fees for office space, equipment, locations, and so on, as well as for the five shooting days—would be down the drain. On top of that was the fact that many of the cast and crew who had signed on to do *this project* had turned down other projects to work on this one and would now be out of work—possibly for months—which, as a manager, I understood is not something to be taken lightly.

Choice two was to salvage the project—something Woody was adamant that we do. That would mean figuring out how to make that work; committing to recasting a leading man as quickly as possible, rebudgeting the film, creatively rescheduling the entire project based on the new circumstances, and reshooting the first week. Speed was critical here—we would be burning through $150,000 a day as we tried to come to a definitive decision. Meaning that unless we made the decision to shut down immediately, we would have to pay for each "shooting day" going forward *even if we weren't shooting anything*, and the next shooting day began roughly twelve hours after that phone call from Bobby Greenhut.

Obviously the five days we had already shot with Keaton were now worthless (we had already spent millions of dollars to get to this point), our burn going forward was substantial, and scores of people were working at dozens of locations building and dressing sets to be ready in accordance with the time frame out-

---

was injured a week into shooting, we would have had insurance to cover it—albeit with a high deductible—but not for a creative decision like this.

lined in the precisely planned—and now equally worthless—shooting schedule.

One look at the magnitude of this problem and I recognized it as a full-blown crisis. Using my numeric scale and rubric, we had a 10, and we needed to *objectify, contain,* and *act.*

Objectify
The smartest move was to protect the millions
of dollars we had already spent
by completing the project.

Contain
Limit any additional loses by leveraging the assets
we had available to us.

I knew that I had to ignore many of the considerations I would normally use as my hard corners in scheduling a film and instead prioritize the work based on a new hard corner—*shoot whatever we can without the lead actor.* That required ignoring additional costs, crew overtime, and normal scheduling practices. I saw that we had a total of nine days of work we could do without the leading man present. If Woody could recast the lead in time to have him on set on day ten, and if we could dress the actors and sets for the 1920s ahead of the original schedule for these nine days of shooting, we could contain the financial loss to the five days we had already shot. *That* was a feasible plan and minimized losses.

After pulling up those scenes that didn't call for the leading man, I effectively scheduled an interim nine-day movie. Remember, because we meticulously break down every scene, I have every detail of the entire movie laid out on the strip board. That meant that when I got that call from Greenhut, I could open the board and in a matter of minutes isolate the specific scenes that did not call for the leading man. By looking at those cardboard strips, I knew exactly how many days this was (nine), which actors were needed, which locations, what special equipment—even what props—we needed to shoot those scenes.

By ignoring all the normal scheduling parameters and using my new hard corner of *shoot all the work without the lead actor*— a very big, overwhelming problem became much simpler to understand and approach logically. I was now basing my solution solely on the feasibility of frontloading the scenes the leading man was absent from, knowing that this was the only option that would tide us over until we had a new actor. From that flowed very specific and defined work for all the individual departments.

Act

Now it was time to execute. With this new hypothetical schedule in front of me, as numerous other people scrambled to do their jobs—talk to the studio, reassure cast, redo location deals, and so on—I scrambled to figure out something we could shoot the following day. Then I reconfigured the call and the next morning had a meeting with all department heads to explain what we had in mind and ask about the feasibility of the plan from each of their perspectives. Coded into these conversations was an enormous amount of *respect*. I was *asking* their professional opinion as to whether they thought we could pull this off, which demonstrated a couple of things to them. First, that management was stepping up and making decisions, and second, that management respected their opinions and understood that we needed them on board to execute the plan. I also had to know if each department *could* pull this off under the new time constraints. *Could casting get the actors we needed on such short notice? Were certain locations available based on our new dates? How long would it take to build, paint, and dress the sets we now needed well ahead of the original schedule?*

Now that we had everyone's input and buy-in, we were able to move forward. Some departments had to work around the clock, others were confident that they could adapt as we went along, and I was able to assess that they were all highly motivated to do so. Part of this was certainly commitment to professional excellence on their part, a big part of it was loyalty to Woody, and for some, it was as simple as the desire to stay on the payroll. Because filmmaking is freelance, as noted earlier, many of these crew members had turned down other jobs to do this one, and if we shut down, it might have meant that they would go months without another film—or paycheck.

Woody screen-tested a number of actors and in short order selected Jeff Daniels to play the dual role of Tom Baxter and Gil Shepherd in the film. Any of the other actors who had been cast for smaller parts who were now not available under the new schedule were recast, as well. Since Michael Keaton is five foot nine and Jeff Daniels is six foot three, none of the costumes that had been built for Michael would fit Jeff, so all new wardrobe for Jeff had to be rebuilt or repurchased. During those nine days, we shot all the scenes without the leading man, and on day ten, Jeff Daniels was on set working. Over the course of the film, we eventually reshot the material from the original five days that we had filmed with Michael Keaton and successfully completed the project—albeit at a higher cost.

In general, using the simple numeric 1–10 grading system, along with identifying the hard corners and employing the rubric to *objectify*, *contain*, and *act*—either alone or in combination—gives a manager much-needed structure and direction that can be very useful in handling everything from a mundane problem to a full-blown crisis. But the rubric to *objectify*, *contain*, and *act* offers something even beyond that much-needed structure and direction.

In a crisis, some degree of control and power is lost by the manager as it shifts to the external forces that caused, and are driving, that crisis—that's part of the reason why we often feel so overwhelmed and helpless in times of crisis—we've lost power and control over outcomes, and we know it. I've found that by *objectifying* a problem, *containing* the damage, and purposefully *acting*, a manager can, in a swift and direct move, invert the control and power away from that external force and return it back to the manager(s) handling a particular crisis. What that means is that when we, as managers, *objectify*, *contain*, and *act*; we are purposefully employing a single line of code that, just like *don't call us, we'll call you* allows us to invert the control and power that we lost at the onset of the crisis and bring it back to ourselves—and doing *that* can dramatically alter outcomes for the better.

Consider that *The Purple Rose of Cairo*—a film that potentially could have fallen apart and not been made—went on to be nominated for, and win, numerous international awards. Jeff Daniels and Mia Farrow were both nominated for the Golden Globe for Best Performance by an actor/actress in a comedy/musical.

Woody was awarded the Golden Globe for Best Screenplay and the film won Best Motion Picture. He received an Oscar nomination for Best Screenplay and won the BAFTA for Best Film and Best Screenplay. The film won the FIPRESCI Prize in Cannes, the César for best foreign film, and was awarded Film of the Year from the London Critics' Circle Film Awards, along with many other industry awards.

Insight:

Not every problem is a crisis, even though it can feel that way.

Action Steps:
Set up your own Richter scale to assess the gravity of individual problems.
When facing a genuine crisis use the rubric—*objectify, contain, and act*—to structure a response.

Result:
Separates the small problems from the big ones.
Stabilizes situations in a very productive, forward-moving manner.
Modulates response and prevents over- or under-reaction.
Provides structure and logical direction for fast and efficient problem and crisis resolution.
Reduces stress and assures better outcomes.

REMEMBER TO LEAD AS WELL AS MANAGE

★

PUT ME IN, COACH . . .

CASE STUDY:
The film *Soup for One*. Warner Bros. Directed by Jonathan
Kaufer; starring Saul Rubinek, Marcia Strassman, and Gerrit
Graham.

IF YOU DO a bit of crisis forensics—say, by conducting a post-
mortem on even a small crisis that *wasn't* managed particularly
well—it usually becomes evident that having a preset plan for
handling it may have led to a more successful outcome. On top of
that, it's pretty much a given that most of us rely on the fact
that those in charge *actually have* a crisis-management plan in
place and that for organizations dealing with large groups of
people, we expect that the plan is far more detailed, comprehensive, and industry specific than my one-size-fits-all-first-line-of-
defense rubric to *objectify*, *contain*, and *act* is. In fact, it's fair to
say that we *expect* that "they"—those nebulous higher-ups who

we *assume* will take care of things—will step up and offer a solution when things go terribly wrong.

When "Sully" Sullenberger crash-landed that US Airways flight in the Hudson River in 2009 after a bird strike during takeoff resulted in a catastrophic loss of power to both engines, the National Transportation Safety Board (NTSB) designated it "the most successful ditching in aviation history." That happened because virtually every person involved had extensive training in how to respond in a situation of this type, and they executed that training flawlessly.*

But perfectly planned and executed responses like that are not always the case. There are literally thousands of examples of catastrophic system-wide failures of leadership, but it only takes recalling one—Hurricane Katrina in New Orleans in 2005—for us to quickly be reminded of what *has* happened when leadership fails. Then consider the 2014 Ebola epidemic when the US government assured us that the health care system was prepared, but the organization National Nurses United interviewed more than four hundred nurses in over two hundred hospitals in twenty-five states and found that 80 percent of the nurses reported that their hospitals had not communicated to them *any* procedural policy regarding how to handle a patient who walked through the door with symptoms of Ebola, and think for a moment about what *could* have happened in that situation if events had unfolded differently.

---

* This list included the captain and flight crew, the NY Waterway ferryboat and Circle Line Sightseeing Cruises boat operators, the New York City Police Department aviation and harbor units, and the New York City Fire Department.

This illustrates that as "simple" as the advice to establish even a basic system of crisis management to fall back on may sound, it's not actually something that is implemented as often as it should be, even with large organizations, and even when the consequences can be dire. And it also suggests that we should be asking more often than we actually do, *who are* they? *And are* they *doing their jobs?*

In many businesses, the elusive "they" can be unidentifiable or absent, or just plain worthless and ineffective, not only when we're trying to identify a source of information (I frequently find myself facing a blank stare after asking crew members, "Who's *they?*" when they come to me saying, "*They* said . . ."), but also when there are broader management and leadership issues. And, as we saw with Katrina, "they" can be missing in times of crisis, as well—which means that more often than we'd like to think, "they" needs to be "us."

As I came up through the ranks, when we were shooting and crew members were at an impasse because management or leadership directives were sorely needed but seemingly absent, occasionally I'd hear someone lightheartedly ask, "Are there any grownups around?" But underpinning that tongue-in-cheek sarcasm was a question rooted in solid ground and astute observation.

Employees understand that they need both *management* and *leadership* in order to do their jobs well, *and they recognize when it's missing.*

And like most managers, I learned *that* lesson the hard way.

VERY EARLY IN my career, I worked as a second assistant director on the Warner Bros. film *Soup for One*, which was directed by

Jonathan Kaufer, a young, first-time director in his midtwenties. It was an interesting film for me for several reasons, including the fact that Kaufer had such a contentious relationship with one of the lead actors—Gerrit Graham—that for much of the shoot they weren't speaking. When the two of them were standing on the set just a few feet apart, I had to stand between them and "translate." Kaufer—whose job it was to direct Gerrit in the scene—would say something to me like, "Tell Gerrit to take an extra beat before he delivers his line on the next take," and I'd turn and say, "Gerrit, take an extra beat before you deliver your line on the next take," and then Gerrit would say, "Tell Jonathan, 'Okay.'" And I'd say . . . well, you get the idea.

This type of relationship between an actor and director is virtually unheard of. It's one that I never witnessed again on a film set and was certainly one that got the wheels turning in my head as I thought about the damaging impact of poor management, the imperative of communication, and the importance of diplomacy.

And the lessons I gleaned from that picture didn't end there.

One day when we were shooting, because of a family medical emergency, the first assistant director—my boss and the person responsible for running the set—had to leave abruptly. As I stepped up to manage the set by myself for the first time—a responsibility that I was not yet quite ready to handle on my own, although I didn't completely understand that—I knew that I had an opportunity to prove myself, and felt that familiar, powerful rush of "Put me in, Coach" adrenaline. Approaching my newly assigned position as "boss for the rest of the day" with enthusiastic vigor, and not wanting to waste any time, I immediately gave the crew the go-ahead to start roughing out the lighting for the upcoming scene.

To give you some background, when we arrive at a new location to film (which occurs almost daily), wherever we are—say, an apartment building, a restaurant, or a street corner—work happens in fairly predictable phases. First, the trucks are unloaded, and then the equipment is carried close to the set where it will be easily accessible. Next, we block and rehearse the first scene with the cast, a process that determines *exactly* where the actors will sit, stand, and move, as well as how the scene will be covered—meaning where the camera will be, what lenses will be used, and what shots we will do.

As I discussed in chapter 2, the process of blocking is an example of extreme task segmentation as the director and cinematographer identify the minute details of movement as well as the desired coverage (e.g., medium shots, close-ups, over the shoulders, inserts, and dolly shots). That information identifies what will be in frame or "seen" by the camera, which in turn defines what we need to light, what we have to dress, and where we can put the equipment along with myriad other nuanced details necessary for filming.

After blocking and rehearsing—since we now know the actors' exact positions and how the scene will be covered, the main lights are hung or placed, spreaders are put up to hang additional lights from, and a very general, broad-strokes lighting scheme is roughed out. Once that's finished, the fine-tuning can be done—any fill lights, accent lights, and backlights are set. During this process, the set is loud and a little chaotic. There may be fifteen or twenty people working simultaneously, talking and shouting over one another in order to be heard as the grips move ladders, electricians haul cables and set lights, set dressers move furniture, and departments like prop and camera move their own pieces of equipment around.

Getting back to my story, in the middle of all of this, Jonathan, the director, told me that he wanted to hold a rehearsal and block the scene. Now, I *should* have known to call for blocking and rehearsing *before* I had the crew start to tear the room apart to light and that most of the work they were doing would have to be redone because I didn't—but I hadn't figured out that mistake yet. So when I panicked a bit, it was, unfortunately, not for the right reason. I was worried that to hold a rehearsal at this point would necessitate stopping the work and clearing the crew and equipment. I still hadn't realized that the crew shouldn't have been lighting at this point *at all*.

I then proceeded to make things worse.

Adding another poor management call on top of the first one, I walked up to the key grip (the grips push camera dollies and set flags and cutters in front of lights, among other things) and, anticipating that he might tell me that they only needed a few more minutes to finish lighting, I very foolishly *asked him* if he thought we should rehearse now or if I should tell Jonathan that we should wait on the rehearsal until they were done lighting. Standing on top of a six-foot ladder, dripping with sweat, he looked down at me with an annoyed expression and responded with a phrase that has stuck with me for thirty-five years.

He said, "You tell me."

The crew needs and expects concrete decisions and direction from above, and it took an event like that for me to truly understand—in a resonates-in-your-bones kind of way—that managers *manage*.

Now you might ask, *Why would the crew care? They're getting paid; so what if they have to redo something?*

The answer is simple: *nobody* respects inefficiency even when they are being compensated well for their work. And it's human nature for employees to not want to be tasked with double work because the person calling the shots doesn't know what he or she is doing. What they *do* respect is a voice of authority saying, "Okay, this is what we're going to do." And whatever that task is, it needs to ring true as being correct, or that manager loses all credibility.

That day when I finally realized that I had failed to provide that, the situation was made all the more painful for me because virtually everyone on set knew that we should *always* rehearse *before* we light. But they weren't about to tell me something that as their manager, *I* should have known.

In this case, my inexperience led to a poor management decision, it wasted time and money (as mentioned, most of the work that grip and electric had done had to be redone *after* the blocking and rehearsal), and it eroded the crew's faith in my ability to manage them going forward. So with my confidence bruised, I cleared the set and held the blocking and rehearsal knowing that I had demonstrated my weakness as a manager in front of the entire crew.

Never one to walk away from a mistake empty-handed, I learned a lesson that was invaluable. Forgetting for a moment the *filmmaking part* of this lesson—*we always block and rehearse before we light*—the management lesson was far more profound. I now understood in an acutely memorable way that my biggest mistake wasn't that I started the lighting work before we blocked; it was asking the key grip what *he* thought we should do.

Determining that was *my* job.

While this was a lesson in the nuance and value of *management* and the propensity for poor decisions and expressions of weakness to erode the tensile strength of the teams we are building, managers also have to recognize the times that call for real *leadership*. Just as that key grip was looking for me to make a decision as a manager, in times of crisis all the workforce will be looking to their manager to *lead*, as well.

THE REASON THAT I find the transition from manager to leader to be so noteworthy is that I've observed that very often when significant issues arise, or at the onset of a crisis, many involved, from those in the highest echelons to the lowliest employees, are hoping that "someone else"—the nebulous "they"—will step up and take the leadership role necessary to solve a particular problem. And there is a whole slew of reasons why we, as individuals, may be prone to holding back from taking control in tough situations—reasons that could be described as a dangerous psychological cocktail that's one part fear of failure, one part self-preservation, and in some cases, one part *loss aversion*. Of course, shying away from a task because of fear of failing, reluctance to "own" the outcome in a high-risk situation that may not turn out well, and concern over losing our jobs is pretty easy for most of us to relate to. But add loss aversion to that mix and you have a downright toxic recipe for potential inaction.

The behavioral economic theory of loss aversion would predict that for someone to willingly step up and volunteer to take over during a crisis in business (one that involves the potential loss of large amounts of money), the perceived potential *gain* of making those tough financial calls would have to outweigh the perceived risk for *loss* by 2–1. And that's because we're prewired to hate acknowledging a loss more than we love to take credit for a gain—twice as much, in fact.

Loss aversion is so powerful that it's often the Achilles' heel of stock market investors who have a propensity to sell winning positions in order to bank the gains—which feels good—and hang on to losing positions to avoid selling and acknowledging a loss—which feels twice as bad. And they'll do this even when market conditions indicate that those buy-sell decisions make no financial sense. That distaste for loss can alter our behavior in decision-making to favor *avoiding loss at all costs*, even when doing so is irrational and self-destructive, and especially in high-risk financial situations.

This reticence to own the consequences and make those tough calls is amplified in businesses where there are siloed departments populated with employees who, because of the underlying corporate structure, have an even greater vested interest in doing nothing when leadership is needed. *Harvard Business Review* reports that this type of institutionalized, systemically supported reticence to step up and make tough calls can lead to zombie projects that are dead in every sense, and yet, due to momentum and the reluctance by everyone involved to take a leadership role and call "time of death," they continue. Just as stock market investors don't want to book a loss, corporate managers generally don't, either. As a result, many projects that are widely known by those working on them to no longer be viable go on—sometimes for years—draining resources and going nowhere, propelled by that dangerous cocktail of fear of failure, self-preservation, and loss aversion made all the more toxic by those corporate silos that foster and drive self-serving agendas.

In filmmaking, even though we have siloed departments, because we correct for them with a common goal and a keystone manager, this plays out very differently. We constantly make *swift, aggressive decisions—even when they involve financial loss.* In fact, we have no choice but to be cutthroat if something isn't working because the cost of continuing in the wrong direction is so great. And learning to do this actually produces a managerial "relief valve." It is highly productive to acknowledge a mistake, correct it, bank the loss, and move forward in a more positive direction. That requires actually having the strength to *lead*, to book those losses when that's the correct decision, whatever business we are in. Doing so frees up valued assets—whether that's financial capital, human capital, or time—and allows us to be in the position to then book gains with newly acquired positions.

What this indicates, though, is that in many businesses and situations, the potential pool of volunteer problem-solvers in any given management situation may be limited—and therefore smaller than you think—since many of those around us won't want to rise to a leadership role and take responsibility for a particular problem because of the fear of owning the outcome if things don't turn out well. Of course, the flip side of this equation is rather compelling; with so many people stepping back, those tough situations and crises offer unique opportunities for managers to step up.

And it's worth reminding ourselves that as managers we have a lot to lose if we *don't* step up and lead. All that equity, tensile strength, and trust we have worked so hard to build with our team can be lost if we're put to the test in those leadership situations and *don't* deliver. I've found that since the rubric to *objectify*, *contain*, and *act* is a structured call to action—one that mandates stepping up with an immediate response—it helps me bypass those normal instincts *to do nothing* when real leadership is needed. I've also found, over years of observation and trial and error, that there are some additional steps beyond *objectify*, *contain*, and *act* that we can take to make sure that when those leadership opportunities arise and we *do* step up, we are better prepared to lead *well*.

FIRST RECOGNIZE THAT LEADERS HAVE TO MANAGE, AND MANAGERS HAVE TO LEAD; THAT THOSE ROLES AREN'T DISCRETE BUT RATHER, FOR MOST OF US, THEY'RE TRANSITIONAL.

As important as being a good manager is, it's also important for managers to understand the key differences between *managing* and *leading* and how those differences manifest in their particular lines of work. For example, in filmmaking, because the life cycle of projects is so short, we have no long-term growth strategies or five-year plans and no corporate vision statements, but we *do* have industry-specific leadership needs. And unlike the highly segmented and clearly defined jobs and tasks that I've been advocating, for many of us, *within our jobs*, the transition between the role of manager and that of leader is, more often than not, *fluid*. In my case, one minute I might be managing, and moments later, I may find myself facing a leadership challenge—often without much time in between. What size trucks are we going to use?[†] Which scenes are we going to do when, and why? What time should we set the call on a particular day, and when do we wrap? Should I authorize additional manpower and equipment? Should we build a set or shoot those scenes at a live location? Those are all *management decisions*. On the other hand, there are decisions to facilitate and accommodate a particular department—say, the wardrobe department when they come to me concerned they won't be ready with the costumes for a particular scene—or the steps I have to take to *instill confidence* by quelling the concerns of a nervous first-time director or insecure actor. Or when I decide to stand at the camera no matter what—even in the freezing cold in the middle of the night when *I could* be inside. Or when I make the conscious decision to always make a statement of respect by making sure that I'm the last guy through the lunch line in the catering tent so the crew members who have been hauling cable and unloading trucks get to sit down and eat first. And all the decisions I make to balance the needs of individuals against the needs of the project as a whole in my role as a keystone manager. All *these efforts* fall under the auspices of *leadership*.

Just as the grip standing on the ladder on *Soup for One* was expecting me to *manage* the workday, he will be looking for me to *lead* in a time of crisis, as well.

[†] For example, union rules dictate that as the trucks get incrementally larger, you have to carry more teamsters. Therefore, you don't want larger trucks than you actually need. These seemingly small management decisions can have a big impact on the transportation budget, which is almost always the largest below-the-line cost on a movie.

WHEN THAT HAPPENS, ACT FAST.

Decisive action is paramount in a crisis, even if you end up making an aggressive mistake. As my old football coach used to say, "If you're unsure who to block, hit anyone." And that concept pertains to business, as well. When you are called to lead, the last thing you want to do is vacillate, show fear, display weakness and indecisiveness, or fail to act. In fact, during a crisis, I've found that in almost all cases, acting quickly produces a more desirable outcome than acting slowly, for one very specific reason. *Crises have momentum.* And at the onset, that momentum is headed in the wrong direction. So even though a leader sets the course of action in play, it's important to remember that it's *the team* that executes it. The force behind the shift in momentum from going in the *wrong* direction to going in the *right* direction comes from a workforce compelled to work hard by leadership they believe in. *That* means it's important to demonstrate that you are making a move to correct the situation before they lose faith in your ability and willingness to do so.

NEXT, RECOGNIZE THAT JUST AS IN YOUR ROLE AS A
MANAGER, AS A LEADER, YOU WILL LIKELY HAVE
CONFLICTING LOYALTIES.

Like most managers, I have split loyalties, and those split loyalties are still there when I am called upon to lead. I have fiduciary responsibility to the studio and the producers to protect the money. I have creative allegiance—and responsibility—to the director to make sure he or she has the opportunity to make the film he or she envisions. And I also have enormous responsibility and professional loyalty to look after the interests of the crew. Filmmaker James Cameron (*Titanic*, *Avatar*) so aptly said, "Filmmaking is war. A great battle between business and aesthetics." And that constant battle between business and aesthetics—between the competing interests of the money and the art—often manifests as differing perspectives, biased agendas, and tough management and leadership calls.

People working in other industries also face similar conflicts of interest and competing allegiances—loyalty split between upper management, board members, investors, stockholders, outside clients, customers, and, of course, the team they are managing, as well as any self-serving interests of their own if their jobs are not structured as keystone positions. A measurement of a *good manager* is someone who can handle the day-to-day issues of scheduling, work flow, and delegation while fostering an atmosphere of high motivation, high productivity, and creative problem-solving with efficiency and decorum. But a measurement of a *good leader* is someone who sees past those day-to-day responsibilities, who understands the shifting nature of his or her loyalties, and who knows who and what to stand up for *and why*.

Always lead with confidence.

Be stalwart in your decisions, be consistent in implementation, and instill confidence in team members when they lose it—because confidence and conviction are *infectious*. Do this consistently as a manager so you are in a better position to lead when you are called to. If you decide to head in one direction, you don't want the troops looking over their shoulders when you're halfway there, wondering if they should turn around and go the other way. This plays out in many ways in filmmaking. For example, since we shoot out of sequence, it means that directors have to direct actors controlling for emotional tone in scenes that may be side by side when the film is cut together but are shot weeks or months apart. They have to be supremely confident in these directorial decisions and communicate that confidence to the actors performing those scenes so they can deliver their best performance. We also do multiple takes and coverage, which means that when we're shooting a comedy, the jokes can feel tired after we've heard them over and over as we shoot. I've seen directors waver and lose confidence in the material and then rewrite because they've panicked and decided the dialogue is no longer funny, simply because they've heard the jokes so many times. Or say we're doing a stunt sequence and we're all set to go; the confidence I exude to everyone involved—from the stuntmen to the director to the crew—is critical for the safe and flawless execution of that gag.

PRACTICE COMPROMISE LIKE IT'S YOUR RELIGION.

There came a time midway through filming *Great Expectations* when the director, Alfonso Cuarón (Academy Award winner for *Gravity*, 2013), was asked by the studio to drop some scenes from the film for budgetary reasons. He was disappointed because those scenes—while technically not necessary for the plot—were important to him, and when he got off the phone with the studio, he said to me, "If I don't shoot myself in the foot, they'll kill my baby." While I respected the fact that, like all directors, his vision for the success of his project was based on *artistry above cost*—a perspective that led him to fight for every foot of film he wanted to shoot—I had even greater respect for the fact that, as the curator of what was both a creative *and* a commercial work, he could see beyond his siloed perspective and *compromise*. Even though he didn't like it, he understood that this was both a commercial and an artistic endeavor and that without compromise he would have no project. That's *real* leadership.

DEFUSE ALL VOLATILE SITUATIONS.

When someone gets hot under the collar—which can be triggered by even small things in high-pressure work situations—I always try to isolate the warring parties. That removes any onlookers and possible embarrassment, which generally allows both parties to save face and removes issues of damaged pride that could make resolution of conflicts all the more difficult. Next, I immediately drop the volume of my voice to a lower-than-normal speaking level when talking to the parties involved in order to further deescalate things. I listen to both sides and then offer a resolution that is reasonable and declare the conflict over—something I try to do with a little joke to remind everyone of how trivial the conflict is in the grand scheme of what we are attempting to do. And conflicts are commonplace on set.

For example, when we rehearse, the actors want the props for the scene we are rehearsing—that can be anything from an umbrella to a lighter to a briefcase—because it adds a bit of "real feel" to their performance. If I'm waiting to do a rehearsal in an apartment on an upper floor of a high-rise with Keanu Reeves, Al

Pacino, Charlize Theron, and Taylor Hackford and the property master isn't upstairs with those props because the location manager sent the elevator up with camera equipment instead of giving the property master priority, then the property master is apt to go ballistic. Even if he's late by three minutes, those three minutes that I'm standing there waiting with Keanu, Al, Charlize, and Taylor can feel like an eternity to all of us. It screams inefficiency; their time is valuable, and nobody wants to be waiting for a few props. That property master knows that and will be fuming because he was made to look bad because the location manager co-opted the elevator. To the outside observer, this is nothing—it's three minutes—but to the property master, it's embarrassing to show up late for the rehearsal—which brings us back to the Oscar Effect—*he really wants to do his job well*. When the rehearsal is over and the propman confronts the location manager, I need to step in and defuse the situation immediately since I need them to be working in concert, not building animosity. When they get things off their chests and finally shake hands, it's just one of the incremental wins that I use to build the tensile strength of the team—by not letting that strength erode.

HAVE HUMILITY.

On one particular picture when we were about to shoot a nude shower scene with our leading lady in a state prison, one of the executive producers who had just flown in from LA was on set for the day, and he sat down in a director's chair by the entrance to the shower room while we were prepping the set and started making phone calls. He continued talking nonstop on his cell phone, apparently completely oblivious to, or selfishly unconcerned about, the fact that he was in the way; nor did he seem concerned with the sensitive nature of what we were about to shoot. The crew set up for the shot by working around him, and when we were ready, I announced that everyone should clear the set. But he didn't leave. He continued to sit there, center stage, talking on his phone. I wasn't sure if he didn't hear me or if he was making a power statement—*I'm important, and I'll do whatever I want*—but either way, I wasn't about to have the actress brought to the set while he was there. So there we were, spending his roughly $20,000 per hour in ninety-degree heat in a maximum-security prison at three in the morning on the verge of blowing the night's work. As "the money," he should have had an eye for efficiency, and as an artistic employer, he should have been bending over backward to make sure that the leading lady felt comfortable and secure, *not uncomfortable and insecure*. He was costing us time and money and showing disrespect for the leading actress, and everyone on the crew knew that—and disrespected *him* for it. He finally got up and left, but not until both the director and I spoke to him personally.

As for what else he communicated to the crew? That was even worse. Through his behavior, he was also communicating loud and clear that he didn't care about time or money and had little respect for the cast or for the hard work the crew was doing. The takeaway for the crew was, *why should we kill ourselves to move faster or be concerned with saving money when he was so willing to waste money?* If this reminds you of the inverse of Ron Friedman's *motivational synchronicity* and the contagious nature of *positive* behavior, it's for a good reason. *Negative behavior is contagious, too.* Not only did this guy interrupt our work flow and display arrogance and disrespect to a key cast member about to perform a sensitive scene, but he also eroded the tensile strength of the crew by creating a motivational sinkhole. And he managed to accomplish all of that in just a few hours on set. He flew out the next day, but the damage was done; I now had a less engaged workforce than I'd had just days prior.

TRUST THE PROCESS.

It's hard for all of us to maintain confidence day in and day out when we are involved in executing difficult tasks, especially if we are sleep deprived and beaten down. My role as a leader is to keep the team focused on the task at hand, on a particular scene or a day's work, understanding that if we get each incremental piece done, and done well, we will finish—and finish well. That requires respect for, and trust in, the process, which circles back to the foundation we laid—to microscheduling, hyperfocus on minute details, segmented jobs, and discrete tasks. On day thirty-seven of a shoot when I look at my board and glance at the call sheet as I face a difficult decision, I have extreme confidence that everything is correct and rarely waver or doubt myself. I *trust the process,* and the fact that all the meticulous planning we did in preproduction, all the specialists hired, the precise scheduling, and the job and task segmentation is a structure I can depend on because *we architected a specific and well-thought-out route to successful execution.* I rely on the fact that if we get the two and a half pages a day of quality footage with great performances that we schedule for each and every day, we will have a completed film at the end of day sixty; one that will be on time, be on budget, reflect the director's vision, and be of the highest creative quality.

MANAGE UP AS WELL AS DOWN.

Most of us are so focused on the fact that we have the employees *under us* to manage and lead that we ignore the fact that some of the toughest and most productive management moves we can make are directed at those occupying the rungs above us. I'm talking about managing strategies directed at *our* bosses. And managing "up" doesn't just mean handling the weak, disruptive higher-ups like that executive producer in the prison; we also have to manage the hardworking, well-qualified people above us, as well.

So just as we need to assess our subordinates (labor force), we also have to examine our superordinates (those above us) and build positive relationships—and equity and trust—with them. When we view our role as managers as working both up and down the vertical hierarchy, we recognize the management opportunities in both directions. That puts us in a better position to work with those higher-ups when things get tough and leadership or support is needed.

AND FINALLY, AS THE PULITZER PRIZE–WINNING PLAYWRIGHT DAVID MAMET WROTE IN *GLENGARRY GLEN ROSS*, AS MANAGERS AND LEADERS WE NEED TO *"ALWAYS BE CLOSING . . ."*

In filmmaking, there is pressure to make decisions quickly and with certitude, and those decisions often have to be sold to a diverse group of people who must sign off on them in rapid succession. And while we all know that salespeople need to *close*, we have to recognize that managers and leaders do, too. In fact, the ability to put together "deals" and sell them to reluctant buyers in a way that will make all parties believe they came out on top is not only the most important part of what salespeople do, it's also the most important part of what leaders and managers do day to day. *Selling and closing improve efficiency and productivity as they move us incrementally forward and demonstrate strength.*

INSIGHT:

Employees want and expect both active day-to-day management and real leadership, and they know when it's missing.

Action Steps:
Lead as well as manage.
Be decisive.
Look for step-up opportunities to lead.
Recognize that you will have conflicting loyalties.
Lead with confidence.
Practice compromise like it's your religion.
Defuse volatile situations.
Have humility.
Trust the process.
Manage above as well as below you.
Always be closing.

Result:

Stronger, more cohesive teams.

Higher efficiency.

Greater chance for positive outcomes.

CONCLUSION: MAKE THE JUMP

———————————————★———————————————

MacArthur Causeway Bridge, Miami Beach

1:00 A.M.

CASE STUDY:
The film *Just Cause*. Warner Bros. Directed by Arne Glimcher; starring Sean Connery, Laurence Fishburne, Kate Capshaw, and Scarlett Johansson.

———————————————————————————————

IT'S JUMP NIGHT.

The blistering south Florida heat has dropped a welcome twenty degrees since we arrived on set for our 5:00 P.M. call when my feet burned through the soles of my sneakers as I stood on the concrete roadway, overseeing the final preparations. We're just minutes away from shooting the final piece of the stunt sequence that I introduced in the opening of this book where we jump a car over the open MacArthur Causeway Drawbridge in the Sean Connery film *Just Cause*. This past week, we shot the lead-in to the jump as the two cars tore through the streets at night, weaving in and out of traffic in a series of high-speed near misses as they made their way up onto the I-47 Causeway that connects Miami Beach to the mainland. It was a complex sequence involving first and second units and filming car to car as well as inside each vehicle after Laurie (played by Kate Capshaw) and her daughter, Katie Armstrong (played by twelve-year-old Scarlett Johansson), were kidnapped from the Eden Roc hotel and forced into a car by Bobby Earl Ferguson, a serial killer played by Blair Underwood. After they left the hotel with Laurie behind the wheel and Bobby holding Katie at knifepoint in the backseat, they raced up Collins Avenue through the city, swerved into oncoming traffic, and then made a run up the wrong side of the causeway with Laurie's husband, Paul (played by Sean Connery), and detective Tanny Brown (played by Laurence Fishburne) in hot pursuit. Tonight, we're slated to shoot the actual jump as the lead car soars over the open drawbridge a hundred feet in the air and then lands hard, but intact, on the far side of the bridge.

When I broke the crew for "lunch" at 11:00 P.M., we'd been setting up for the jump for six hours. It's now 1:00 A.M., we've been "back in" for an hour, and I'm standing with camera operator Ray De La Motte next to the A-camera* on the Miami Beach side of the now locked and open drawbridge—and we're just about ready to go. Operators on thirteen strategically placed cameras are

---

* The *A-camera* is the main camera used when filming. Additional cameras, if used, are designated as *B-camera*, *C-camera*, and so forth.

standing by waiting for me to call, "Roll it," and the stunt driver is in first position about three hundred yards from the bridge opening. He's just minutes away from roaring up the causeway, passing his visual marker at the designated takeoff speed—70 mph—blasting past the point of no return, and launching the car over the open span of the bridge. Once airborne, he'll sail roughly eight stories above the water of Biscayne Bay with the nose of the car elevated for the first few seconds of his five-second flight, reach the far side of the bridge with the nose of the car angled down, and then descend onto the ramp by planting the front and then rear tires firmly on the opposing leaf of the open bridge in an explosion of sparks, at which point he'll recover control of the vehicle, tear down the ramp, and speed away.

Consider that so far this one and seven-eighths–page chase sequence has taken us over a week to shoot—*a period of time in which we'd normally film twenty pages.* And tonight, we'll shoot only scene 127, which is *two sentences* in the script that effectively say: *Laurie's car, pursued by her husband Paul's, jumps over the open drawbridge and gets away.* So as I'm standing on the shoulder of the bridge, contemplating the final details of what is a logistically complicated and dangerous stunt only minutes away from execution, I know that when the chase sequence that we shot this past week is cut together with the bridge jump we'll film tonight, despite the sum total of what we accomplished in our eight days of shooting and the $1.3 million we spent to get it, it will represent only a tiny piece of our finished product; under three minutes of screen time, or less than 3 percent of our $60 million, 102-minute feature film.

I also know that if the bridge jump ends in a catastrophic failure, if someone gets injured or killed, or even if we "just" don't make the night's work and fail to get the shot, much of the responsibility will fall on me. And as I stand on the bridge, looking out over the water, reflecting on the magnitude of what we are about to undertake, and considering just how singularly unique, how painstakingly deconstructed and parsed, and often high risk the process of filmmaking is, I note that at this particular, very brief moment, my surroundings seem, under the circumstances, uncharacteristically calm and quiet.

Eerily quiet.

There are, of course, specific reasons for this. *I am standing in the middle of a shut-down highway.* All the roads and ramps feeding onto the MacArthur Causeway on both sides of Biscayne Bay were completely closed by Miami-Dade County Police eight hours ago. So there are no cars or trucks—and no people, either. Even though this stunt took months of planning to set up, as well as the efforts of hundreds of people *tonight alone*, all unnecessary crew personnel are now off the set, as well. And because we won't "see" inside the car when we film the jump, we have no need for makeup, hair, or wardrobe personnel, and there are no props, set dressers, or soundmen[†] needed for this shot, either. In fact, despite the enormous collaborative effort it took us to get to this point, this shot requires no cast and no extras, and the bulk of the crew is now sitting tight back at base camp. The (relative) handful of people who will be directly involved in the actual filming are now

---

[†] Because we are shooting with an aerial unit (which is loud), recording ambient sound would be pointless.

spread out over our quarter-mile-long set communicating over walkie-talkies.

But there's an additional reason for the quiet. Because of the magnitude of the stunt we're about to do, instead of incrementally shooting lots of coverage and doing multiple takes with a *single* camera like we do for most scenes, we're getting all the coverage we need tonight by filming the jump in one take using *multiple* cameras. Which means that after we execute and film the jump once, there'll be nothing left *to do*. So even though we haven't shot a single frame of film yet, at this point, our work is virtually done—there are no additional shots for the crew *to* set up for. It's what we call the *LFS*—the last fucking shot. In fact, in this case, it's the first *and* last fucking shot; once we do this one, we pack up and go home.

And it will be over *fast*.

While there's a meticulous and time-consuming lead-in to a shot like this, there's a rapid, *don't blink or you'll miss it* execution, too.

The actual shot itself will take all of *twenty seconds*.

Start to finish.

Standing in the quiet of the bridge, as I look to my left, I can see the soft glow of lights from South Beach in the distance. To my right is the silhouette of the Miami skyline. And as peaceful as it is right now, in a few minutes when I send the chopper up into the air to its first position for the aerial shot, it'll be loud— *can't-think, can't-hear, bone-rattling chopper loud*.

But first, I'll communicate one last time with all the key players—the director, Arne Glimcher,[‡] the director of photography,

---

[‡] Director and producer of *The Mambo Kings* and producer of *Gorillas in the Mist*.

Lajos Koltai,[§] the A-camera operator, Ray De La Motte,[**] the driver, the stunt coordinator, the camera crews, the helicopter pilot, and my production staff, along with the police and rescue teams to confirm that they're all good to go. Once the chopper is airborne, right before we shoot the jump, the stunt driver will take a couple of dry runs as rehearsals. He'll stomp on the accelerator and blast up the ramp, but this time—because it's practice—just before he reaches the launch point, he'll brake hard, stopping the car just short of the open bridge leaf and the actual jump. He'll use these practice runs to judge speed and control, see how the car responds, choose a driveline, set some visual markers, and designate a point of no return. The camera crews will use these test runs to adjust framing and practice their movements as they pan with him. The camera operators positioned to film the jump itself—or the flight—as well as those designated to film the landing on the far side of the bridge will have to rely on what *we think* the car's flight path and landing position will be and adjust framing, incrementally, on the fly. There'll be no practice runs on the actual jump or the touchdown and getaway, and no guarantee the driver will put down exactly where we think he will.

All night, Arne, Lajos, Ray, and I, along with the camera crews, have been laying out the logistics—desired coverage and ideal camera positions and selecting frame lines and shot sizes. The A-camera is easy to set because it's always positioned for the most important shot—or in some cases the most difficult shot—and tonight it is positioned to capture the whole span of the jump, from

[§] A world-class Hungarian cinematographer who has shot over sixty feature films and was nominated for an Academy Award for *Melina*.

[**] Camera operator on *The Witches of Eastwick*, *Lethal Weapon 2*, *The Prince of Tides*, *Batman Forever*, and dozens of other top-feature films.

launch to landing. But it took us a couple of hours to lay out the grid for the other cameras. With this much equipment to position, it gets complicated, not just from the standpoint of framing but for lighting, as well. We positioned one camera to just capture the landing. Another to get a tight shot of the car at launch. Yet another to catch a frontal shot as it roared up the open drawbridge.[††]

Over the course of the night, I continually check with each separate department for updates; it's a slow, incremental, and siloed process for everyone. I get updates from the gaffer and time projections on lighting. But the lighting can't be fine-tuned until after 9:15 P.M. when it's dark, so the night lumbers on.

The stunt team has double-checked the safety details of the car. The lighting has been completed—a complex job that involved laying miles of cable, bringing in additional generator trucks, and setting up dozens and dozens of lights, and my production staff has been going over street and road lockups. I've been working side by side with all departments, incrementally fine-tuning the execution and management of the event with the goal of getting the best possible footage while simultaneously keeping my eye on organization, strategy, timing, communication, budget, and, of course, safety.

Even though we have assembled a team of experts to do this gag, the risk is not small. All week long as we filmed the car chase, we faced the potential for myriad complications and mishaps— both the possibility of technical snafus and human error—head-on collisions, unintended sideswipes, equipment failure—the list of

---

[††] The cameras also had to be positioned so they wouldn't be seen by (or in the shot of) any of the other cameras.

possible problems was virtually endless. There were intricate camera rigs, insert cars, multiple vehicles, and multiple stunt drivers. Then there was the safety of the cast and crew—including our twelve-year-old actress, Scarlett Johansson—the possibility for civilian injuries, breached perimeters on our locked-down streets, property damage, and even death. And tonight, there's the possibility of a failed jump that would leave us with a car and stunt driver careening at high speed toward the waters of Biscayne Bay.

As cool as a stunt may look on-screen, the danger in executing a shot like this can't be overstated. The margin of error is razor thin, lives hang in the balance, and there are a staggering number of codependent moving pieces. And stunts like this don't always work out well. Sadly, the film industry has a long history of stunt accidents and stunt-related deaths. The stunt double for Daniel Radcliffe on the *Harry Potter* movies fractured his neck and became paralyzed while performing a gag for the sixth film in the series. A cameraman on *The Dark Knight* (starring Christian Bale as Batman) was killed while doing an action sequence on that film. Brandon Lee died when he was hit by a projectile during a gunshot sequence while filming *The Crow*. Vin Diesel's stunt double was killed on the set of *Triple X (xXx)* while flying in a high-speed paraglider. Pilot Art Scholl died during the filming of *Top Gun* in an aerial stunt sequence. Vic Magnotta, a highly experienced stuntman with whom I worked on a number of pictures in New York, died (on *Skip-Tracer*,‡‡ a film I didn't work on) when the roof of the stunt car collapsed in on him on impact when he drove into the Hudson River. In fact, there were thirty-seven stunt-related

‡‡ Released by TriStar Pictures as *The Squeeze*.

deaths—to say nothing of injuries—on film sets in the decade between 1980 and 1990—65 percent of which involved helicopters. And that *wasn't* an unusual decade.

I know that the safe execution of the bridge jump and the successful filming of it from both a technical and creative standpoint is dependent on the expertise of the entire workforce—the stunt coordinator and driver, the camera crew, production staff and director, as well as the professional efforts of the police and rescue teams. But I also know that the safe execution and creative excellence of our shot will be dependent not just on *individuals* and *individual talent* but also on the aggregate tensile strength of our entire team. And that means that our success tonight is predicated to a large degree on my performance as a keystone manager—*a manager who has no personal agenda other than the success of the project as a whole, eyes on the big picture, and the power to act.*

At this point, in the protracted process of getting a shot that began long before we showed up to film tonight, I'd already done a large part of my job as manager and leader necessary to get us to optimum execution. I'd established a high level of bilateral trust with the crew, leveraged the fact that we have a highly motivated workforce with segmented jobs—and made sure that each and every member of this crew had well-defined, incremental, sequential tasks to accomplish throughout the process. I'd already built equity with the workforce, exploited diversity of skill set, accommodated employees, and isolated the specific relevant hard corners that frame our work. I also arrived on set knowing that I have unwavering respect for process and will practice deliberate calm. I know for a fact that before I yell, "Roll it!" and "Action!" that I will have a clear system of command and control, tightly bounded information flow, and a rock-solid crisis-management plan in place should things go south. And on a night like this with so much at risk, I have also stepped up very deliberately to not only function at the highest level in the role of *manager* but also to function at the highest level in the role of *leader*. I also know that since my system of management is purposefully designed to invert control away from processes and procedures that tend to automate system-wide inefficiencies and direct it *toward* processes and procedures that automate system-wide successes, we will come together tonight as the highest-functioning team we can possibly be.

In order to get to this level of functionality, it meant that for all the months we spent preparing for this sequence, I wasn't thinking about the tedium of the planning and coordination or the difficulty of managing the hundreds of people that this sequence would entail. I wasn't thinking about the money needed to pull off this stunt or who was the weakest link. Rather, I was thinking about building the *tensile strength* of the production team, focusing on how well we were organized and individually trained, what our collective assets were, how well we worked together, and how much trust the crew had in both process and leadership.

When I deconstruct the lead-in and execution to a stunt like this, I know that it involves meticulous planning on three separate but interconnected planes. There's *the execution of the stunt itself, the process of filming it,* and *the overall management of the entire event.* It involves not just flying a car over a bridge but creative vision by the director and cinematographer, and in order to capture that vision to the highest degree on film, it also requires a high level of professional and technical execution of that vision by a talented, well-managed crew and extended workforce. With all the unique elements required, I had to acknowledge that executing this shot was complicated *on all three of these vectors*— from a performance standpoint (stunt driver, car modifications, driving skill), from a filmmaking standpoint (camera angles, lenses, frame lines, lighting, aerial unit), and from a management perspective (strategy, organization, coordination, communication, control).

For the stunt driver, there's a lot involved in a stunt jump like this—it's not just hotshot bravado. It requires professional-level precision driving, honed skill, engineering, athleticism, hot and cold cognition, rapid-fire decision-making, and the ability to maintain calm under pressure. And there's more to it than you might think. Careful consideration is given to the car's make and model, there are elaborate and gag-specific modifications made to the vehicle—shocks, tires, drive train, gas tank—and specialized equipment—safety harnesses, steel cages, and fuel cells (to replace the gas tanks and lessen the chance of fire and explosion on impact), just to name a few. Then there's weight distribution, launch speed and angle, and the driver's midair handling, which all affect "flyability" and trajectory. The car will nose up on launch if the driver accelerates on takeoff and nose down if he's decelerating. Each single mile-per-hour increase in speed at launch incrementally extends the length of flight, which increases the distance between the takeoff and landing points. This kind of stunt takes years of training to master and requires extensive driving experience and knowledge of car mechanics, basic physics, and aerodynamics.

From the standpoint of filmmaking, there's the logistics;

dealing with the planning—the cities of Miami and Miami Beach (police, permits, scheduling . . .).§§ The hiring of top talent, acquiring vehicles, budgeting, hotels, per diem, travel . . . But most important, there's the creative end of filmmaking to consider. That's because it's not just the stunt driver or the stunt itself that creates the drama in a scene like this. It's how we film it—coverage, framing, camera speed—how it's lit, choreographed, edited, and how music and sound effects are added in postproduction, as well. To build drama in the bridge jump, we needed a lot of coverage—wide shots and close-ups and quick cuts of the takeoff and landing. And for the entirety of the chase sequence we did this week, we needed high-speed segments of both the lead car and the chase car, alone and together. We needed near misses, quick starts and stops, insert shots of screeching tires, and the actors' faces showing emotion and fear. Shooting an abundance of drama-building coverage allows the director and editor to intercut short segments of film, and it is those fast cuts that create visual energy and drama that is just as much a driver of suspense as the stunt itself. When we shoot, *we are manufacturing the incremental, component parts of our product.*

A stunt like this is designed to elicit an adrenaline spike in the audience—an eyes-riveted-to-the-screen, sucks-the-air-out-of-the-room, oh-shit, how-did-they-do-that, it's-so-cool, high-adrenaline, big-screen moment. And the real stunt-viewing aficionados want the real thing—not a computer-generated,

---

§§ Despite having to make numerous accommodations, the cities of Miami and Miami Beach rolled out the red carpet for us. A Sean Connery movie is good PR for any city. Plus, we spent millions of dollars when we were there; a film company is really good for the local economy.

impossible-to-execute-in-the-real-word version of high-tech movie magic. They want something that will leave them awestruck in a firestorm of veritable wonderment, and it's always better if the stunt feels authentic and is, at least, *theoretically possible* to execute under the known laws of physics and aerodynamics. Sam Mendes, the director of *Skyfall*, had Daniel Craig (as James Bond) on top of a *real train*—not a computer-generated one. Marc Webb, director of *The Amazing Spider-Man*, *often* used stuntmen on wires and winches—not CGI for the climbs and falls. *Mad Max: Fury Road* used minimal CGI, and the director, George Miller, worked with up to 150 stuntmen at a time in over 300 sequences, and that film won the Oscar for Best Special Effects in 2016. So when we plan and film stunts like these, we're aiming to deliver that big-screen moment; one that will evoke a visceral response worthy of the plotline, the caliber of the cast, the dollars we spent, the time we invested in the project—*and* the most sophisticated movie fans.

On top of all that, there's also the day-to-day operations. The planning, organization, and *management* of all facets of this entire sequence—which for me is a process that always starts with identifying and then building a management path based on the salient, defining hard corners of the project.

ONE OF THE primary hard corners for this entire film *was the stunt sequence* itself, simply because it was one of the most difficult pieces of this project to shoot—and I determined that when I first read the script months before we began principal photography. I knew that we needed to set a hard date for the chase sequence and bridge jump well in advance so we could coordinate with the cities of Miami and Miami Beach to put a plan in place for permission, permits, rerouting traffic, shutting down roads, putting additional police officers on duty, and so on, all of which was flawlessly handled by producer Steve Perry. With an eye toward building tensile strength, I purposely scheduled the stunt sequence for our ninth week of shooting so that our crew—comprised of men and women from New York, Los Angeles, and Miami, could get used to working with each other and gel. That single scheduling decision gave me definitive direction for the entire film since once we locked in the dates for the stunt that became a hard corner for scheduling the rest of the fifty-three-day shoot.

I then had to consider *the specific hard corners for the car chase and bridge jump*. And that at least was easy; the unequivocal, overriding hard corner for the stunt was *safety first, safety always*.

And that framed everything going forward.

With *safety first, safety always* as my hard corner, it became a filter through which all our advance decisions were made, and it also lessened the possibility that I would make a wrong decision in the heat of the moment when I was engaged in very fluid, think-and-respond, live-action management.

Of course, there were a number of other hard corners for the stunt sequence beyond safety:

- *We had to shoot this sequence practically (on location) and at night.* While this may seem obvious, it has significant trailing repercussions. Because the sequence was written as a night exterior, that meant we would be out in the elements on real streets with real weather conditions facing numerous variables outside of our control. Plus, shooting at night meant more complicated and time-consuming lighting. I also had to consider that it rained virtually daily in Florida during the summer, which could potentially shut us down for an hour or more each night, and with a sequence this complex and a unit as big as ours, it would be impractical to try to move to a cover set in the middle of the night even if it *did* rain—so I had to schedule enough days to account for delays.

- *We would only have seven hours of darkness each night to get our work.* Miami in July isn't dark enough to film until 9:15 P.M., and the sun is up at about 4:00 A.M., and that provided us with a seven-hour work window, which included a one-hour meal break, cutting our typical shooting day short.

- *This two-page stunt sequence would take eight days (nights) to complete.* So even though we typically shoot two and a half pages of dialogue a day, because we needed a lot of coverage to build drama in a sequence like this, "averages" went out the window.

- *The jump was too dangerous to shoot multiple times.* So we'd get the coverage we needed by running multiple cameras, which meant hiring—and managing—multiple camera crews. *We'd basically do the jump once and shoot the shit out of it.*

- *For the chase, we'd also have to shoot both picture cars (the lead and chase car) twice.* Once with the principal actors and once with the stunt drivers and stunt doubles so that when edited together it would appear that the actors were in the speeding cars weaving through traffic and jumping over the bridge.

- *Scarlett Johansson was a minor, which meant that she could only work eight hours each night—portal to portal***—and had to be back at the hotel by midnight.* And those eight hours had to include time for travel to and from her hotel, a one-hour meal break, and makeup, hair, and wardrobe time. So her effective filming window would be from 9:15 P.M. (when it got dark) to approximately 11:30 P.M.—or two hours and fifteen minutes.†††

Once the dates were set in place and these hard corners identified, we could then start locking in all the other elements: the number of stuntmen needed, hiring an aerial unit and additional crew, and arranging for equipment (additional generators, lights, camera packages)—along with numerous other considerations, all of which had to be identified, agreed upon, booked, and transported to Miami for those predetermined dates.

Next, we had to find all our specific locations and determine a shooting order. What scenes would be shot first unit, and which would be handled by a second unit? We then decided to shoot as much of the chase as we could in sequence (which helps in terms of continuity and lighting setups). Then we had to scout the locations and work with the director to actually physically map the exact path that our picture cars would take during the chase and

---

*** *Portal to portal* is a term from the Screen Actors Guild contract mandating that actors' work time begins and ends with their pickup and drop-off at the hotel.
††† Parenthetically, had it not been summer, we would have been obligated to tutor her for three hours every day, as well—which could have diminished her work hours even further.

determine the number of shots necessary at each location. That allowed us to more accurately estimate lighting and performance time.

From that, I extrapolated a time frame and determined that we needed one full night at the exterior of the Eden Roc Miami Beach hotel, one full night of the picture cars photographed from the exterior as they drove up Collins Avenue and veered onto Fifth Street through oncoming traffic, and one full night racing up the MacArthur Causeway. Another full night would be required for the stunt sequence of the cars screaming into oncoming traffic just before the open drawbridge and yet another full night to do all the interior dialogue scenes in the lead car with Kate, Blair, and Scarlett (doing all Scarlett's coverage first to get her wrapped since she had restricted work hours). One additional full night was needed to do all the coverage inside the car with Sean and Fish, then one full night for the jump itself, followed by an additional night of second-unit driving and insert shots, and later, a few "pickup" shots of Sean driving with the car on a soundstage utilizing rear projection.

By laying the sequence out in this much detail, we took a big, overwhelming task and parsed it down into incremental, executable segments that made it manageable. The locations were then "tech scouted" with all key personnel—which means that all department heads traveled to the site with the director, DP, and me to determine any department-specific physical and logistical needs and issues. We could then get to work on the other details. And since bad weather—beyond a nightly rainsquall—could occur (July is the start of hurricane season in Florida and the Caribbean), we also had a preplanned contingency date for the following week that was scheduled and agreed to by everyone involved.

CONCLUSION: MAKE THE JUMP

So during those moments right before the jump, just as I first had done early in my career and had done so many times since, as I reflect on what we are about to do, I am acutely aware of the fact that for the night to go well, for me to be able to do my discrete and segmented job of *manager* and *leader* to the best of my ability, I have to have two distinct sets of finely honed skills:

Advanced and sophisticated knowledge of feature filmmaking.

And superlative leadership and management skills.

And I know all too well that it is the management side of those requirements that has been far tougher to learn and is always far tougher to execute. But as I look out over Biscayne Bay in that single final moment before we execute our shot, I know with absolute certitude that we have a team with the tensile strength to pull it off. I know that we have all the elements outlined in this book working for us. And at 1:00 A.M., as I am about to lock it up and call, "Roll it," confidence is high.

Not just mine, but everyone's.

WHEN WE'RE BACK in from lunch at 1:00 A.M., I check with the stunt coordinator to see how things are progressing. He tells me that they're all set.

Before I send the helicopter up and execute the practice runs, I hold a final safety meeting. I instruct everyone, including the camera crews, that once I call action, there's no going back unless the driver aborts. I don't want to hear that the C-camera has a dead battery or film jam after I roll it. If anyone has a camera malfunction or technical problem, it's too bad. We're not abandoning the shot. With multiple camera crews, I know some are better than others, but the concept of the weakest link doesn't concern me. I know that as a whole team, even if there's a malfunction or a bad take on one camera, we'll have enough footage to edit a compelling sequence together. Besides, at a certain point, as the driver nears the open bridge, he can't physically stop the car anyway—he's going.

At the safety meeting, I go over all the logistics and confirm that there are to be absolutely no personnel on the bridge. I ask all department heads if they are ready, with special focus on the stunt coordinator and driver. I check with Ray De La Motte multiple times and then meet with the camera crews and review protocol. I have a final meeting with the director, the DP, the stunt coordinator, and the driver. The point of this meeting is to confirm that we are set *creatively* and that all safety precautions are in place from their perspectives. I ask each of them, one final time, if there are any questions or concerns. Everyone verbally signs off that they are ready—including the helicopter pilot.

Everyone's set. It's a go.

I return to my position on the bridge.

I confirm lockup and that the cameras are set. I confirm that Arne and Lajos, who will monitor the shot via video feed, are ready. I check in with the stunt coordinator and driver one last time. I then communicate with the bridge operator and confirm that the bridge is locked and set. He confirms that he won't change it or do anything unless he hears directly from me only. I confirm that the EMTs and ambulances are in position and the safety boat is in the water on standby by the bridge.

Up until this point, there has been completely open communication—I wanted to hear from everyone about everything. But right before we execute, I shut down that all-inclusive communication system. That means that just like I did for the helicopter scene on *The Prince of Tides*, the walkies will become "listening devices only" for just about everyone so I have open lines and no distractions. From this point forward, I want to make sure that the key players can hear me and are not distracted by unnecessary communication. To do that, I have three separate walkies to handle all the communication I need. I can't be fiddling with channels, so I'm working with multiple devices. I put all the camera crews on a separate channel on one walkie. I have a second walkie for me to talk to my production staff, police, and the picture car, and a third radio for the helicopter pilot. And I have new "hot batteries" and backup walkies standing by, as well. I am the communication conduit. This is very much a siloed endeavor. The driver in the car has no information about the camera placement or lighting. The operator on the B-camera getting the shot of a particular angle of the car landing has limited information about other camera placement. They rely on me to have eyes on the whole picture and make decisions that are correct, dependable—and safe. Throughout the entire process, I am deliberate and calm—and that calm proliferates and builds confidence.

When I determine we are ready from the keys (department heads), I announce, "This is picture. Lock it up . . . Everybody off the air . . . Stand by in the picture car . . ." And finally, "Roll it!"

We get slates (scene number and take). Then I wait for Ray to reframe and refocus. Seconds later, he confirms he's "camera ready" and I call, "Action."

All cameras are now rolling.

On "Action," the stunt driver floors it. From my position on the bridge, I watch him tear up the roadway, approach the ramp, hit his speed, reach the launch point, and soar a hundred feet above the water. *One, one thousand, two, one thousand . . .* He's airborne for about five seconds—just as anticipated—and then sticks the landing.

Once the driver regains control of the car, he continues speeding down the causeway toward Miami as planned. We keep rolling until his car is far off in the distance and I yell, "Cut!"

And there it is: a meticulous and time-consuming lead-in with rapid, *don't blink or you'll miss it* execution. Months of planning, hundreds of workers, and thousands of man-hours of labor, and it's over in twenty seconds.

I radio the picture car and confirm verbally that the driver is fine.

Even though I could see the car the whole time, it's still reassuring to hear the stunt driver's voice. I tell the bridge operator to lower the leaves, and minutes later, the stuntman's driving back to base camp.

I call, "Check the gates,"[‡‡‡] and then we review the footage on a monitor.

It's picture-perfect, and Arne and Lajos are happy.

There will be no need for a second take.

It's just shy of 2:00 A.M. when it's over.

[‡‡‡] All the first assistant camera operators check that there isn't a piece of hair or dust in the film gate, which would render the film unusable and report back that "the gate's good."

Only forty-seven minutes from when I was standing on the bridge in awe of the quiet, over the air, I say, "Thanks for a great night, everybody. It's a wrap," and start walking down the empty causeway back to base camp. I shake a few hands along the way as my staff distributes the call sheets for the next shooting day.§§§

That's it.

Nothing particularly special happens at the wrap. It's the wee hours of the morning, and it's been a long week. I get into a car with Arne and Lajos and head back to the hotel. It will take about an hour for the crew to load out of this location, and then it's back to their hotels for all of them, too.

As tough as this shot was, and as much as it cost in time and money, it was the cap to a key dramatic sequence in the movie. So getting it was slow but important forward progress.

This week, we had manufactured just under three minutes of screen time.

And tonight, all of five seconds.

But that is filmmaking; and when all is said and done, for all of us, it's been just another day at the "office."

A few weeks from now, on the last day of shooting when we wrap principal photography on this film, everyone on the crew will be headed somewhere else. Either to a new project in a new city— or new country—with a largely new crew, or back home to wait for the phone to ring. I know that wherever I go next, and no matter what challenges I face, I will bring with me both an

---

§§§ The call sheet is issued each day by my department and indicates when and where to show up for work, what we'll be filming, and other specific information.

advanced and sophisticated knowledge of feature filmmaking and a hard-earned and fire-tested system of leadership and management based on the Hollywood principle and inversion of control that will make my job a whole lot easier and our outcomes a whole lot better.

I will have my Hollywood MBA to guide me.

And if it works for me as we light guys on fire and fly cars over open bridges, just imagine what inverting control, building tensile strength and trust, creating your own Oscar Effect, accommodating your workforce, building equity you can cash in, exploiting diversity, finding the hard corners, adopting a crisis-management model, and always remembering to lead as well as manage can do to create better outcomes for you in your business—whatever that may be.

NOTES

---★---

PREFACE

Bond, Paul. "Study: Global Entertainment Industry Poised to Top $2 Trillion in 2016." Hollywood Reporter. June 5, 2013.

INTRODUCTION

Adkins, Amy. "Only 35% of U.S. Managers Are Engaged in Their Jobs." Gallup Business Journal. April 2, 2015. http://www.gallup.com /businessjournal/182228/managers-engaged-jobs.aspx.

Davidson, Adam. "Building a Harley Faster." *New York Times*. January 28, 2014.

Garvin, David A. "How Google Sold Its Engineers on Management." *Harvard Business Review*. December 2013.

Green, Alison. "Why Are There So Many Bad Managers? The Seven Top Reasons Being the Boss Is So Difficult." *US News and World Report*. November 11, 2013.

Kotler, Steven. "Cognitive Warming: Brain Training for High Pressure Decision-Making." *Forbes*. September 17, 2014.

State of the American Workplace: Employee Engagement Insights for U.S. Business Leaders. Washington, D.C.: Gallup, 2013.

CHAPTER 1: INVERT CONTROL

Fowler, Martin. "InversionOfControl." Martin Fowler.com. June 26, 2005. http://martinfowler.com/bliki/InversionOfControl.html.

Mead, Matthew. "Hollywood Principle—Don't Call Us, We'll Call

You!" MatthewMead.com. November 8, 2008. http://matthewtmead
.com/blog/hollywood-principle-dont-call-us-well-call-you-4/.

Chapter 2: Begin to Build Tensile Strength

Bhalla, Vikram, Jean-Michel Caye, Andrew Dyer, Lisa Dymond, Yves
Morieux, and Paul Orlander. *High-Performance Organizations: The
Secrets of Their Success.* Boston: Boston Consulting Group, September 2011.

Dickstein, B. D., C. P. McLean, J. Mintz, L. M. Conoscenti, M. M.
Steenkamp, T. A. Benson, W. C. Isler, A. L. Peterson, and B. T. Litz.
"Unit Cohesion and PTSD Symptom Severity in Air Force Medical
Personnel." *Military Medicine* 175, no. 7 (July 2010): 482–6.

"Paper Table." PBS Kids. http://pbskids.org/designsquad/parentsedu-
cators/resources/paper_table.html.

Pentland, Alex. "The New Science of Building Great Teams." *Harvard
Business Review.* April 28, 2012.

Rath, Tom. *StrengthsFinder 2.0.* 1st ed. New York: Gallup Press, 2007.

Chapter 3: Engineer Epic Trust

Amabile, Teresa, and Steven J. Kramer. "The Power of Small Wins."
Harvard Business Review. May 2011.

Building Workplace Trust: Trends and High Performance: *2014–2015.*
Boston: Interaction Associates, 2014.

Porath, Christine. "Half of Employees Don't Feel Respected by Their
Bosses." *Harvard Business Review.* November 19, 2014.

Weick, Karl. "Small Wins: Redefining the Scale of Social Problems."
American Psychologist 39, no. 1 (January 1984): 40–49.

Chapter 4: Replicate the "Oscar Effect"

"Andrew M. Thompson, Proteus." *New York Times.* Corner Office.
http://projects.nytimes.com/corner-office/interviews/teamwork
/topic.

Bryant, Adam. "Maynard Webb, Yahoo's Chairman: Even the Best Teams
Can Be Better." *New York Times.* Corner Office. January 3, 2015.

Bryant, Adam. "Speak Frankly, but Don't Go 'Over the Net.'" *New York Times*. Corner Office. September 17, 2011.

Cook, James. "Uber's Internal Charts Show How Its Driver-Rating System Actually Works." *Business Insider*. February 11, 2015.

"The Essentials of High Performance Organizations." American Marketing Association. October 6, 2014. http://www.amanet.org/training /articles/The-Essentials-of-High-Performance-Organizations.aspx.

Friedman, Ron. "Mimicry, Motivation, and How Company Culture Gets Built One Face at a Time." *Psychology Today*. August 29, 2012.

"Job Openings and Labor Turnover Survey." United States Department of Labor Bureau of Labor Statistics. 2014. http://www.bls.gov/jlt/.

"Recipe for Success: Calif. Eatery's Way to Give All Staff Benefits." *NBC Nightly News*. February 17, 2015.

Tabrizi, Behnam. "75% of Cross-Functional Teams Are Dysfunctional." *Harvard Business Review*. June 23, 2015.

CHAPTER 5: ACCOMMODATE EMPLOYEES

Bort, Julie. "LinkedIn Is Giving Its Employees 'Unlimited' Vacation Plus 17 Paid Holidays." *Business Insider*. October 10, 2015.

Cialdini, Robert B., and David A. Schroeder. "Increasing Compliance by Legitimizing Paltry Contributions: When Even a Penny Helps." *Journal of Personality and Social Psychology* 34, no. 4 (October 1976): 599–604.

"Facebook, Apple Pay to Freeze Employees' Eggs." CNNMoney. October 14, 2014. http://money.cnn.com/2014/10/14/news/companies /facebook-apple-egg-freeze/.

"How a No-Tipping Policy Helped This Restaurant Triple Profits in 2 Months." *Fortune*. June 11, 2015.

Lev-Ram, Michal. "No More Pump and Dump: IBM Plans to ship Employees' Breast Milk Home." *Fortune*. July 13, 2015.

Lucchesi, Paolo. "Zazie in Cole Valley to Convert to Tipless, All-Inclusive Model." *SFGate*. May 28, 2015.

NPR. August 10, 2015. http://www.npr.org/sections/thetwo-way/2015 /08/10/431273033/netflix-still-facing-questions-over-its-new-parental -leave-policy.

Paid Time Off Programs and Practices. Scottsdale, AZ: WorldatWork, September 2014.

Pink, Daniel. *Drive: The Surprising Truth About What Motivates Us.* New York: Riverhead Books, 2009.

Sanders, Sam. "Netflix Still Facing Questions Over Its New Parental Leave Policy."

Schwartz, Barry. *The Paradox of Choice: Why More Is Less.* New York: Ecco, 2003.

Silverman, Rachel Emma. "The Price of Unused Vacation Time: $224 Billion." *Wall Street Journal.* May 4, 2015.

Thaler, Richard H., and Cass R. Sunstein. *Nudge: Improving Decisions about Health, Wealth, and Happiness.* New York: Penguin Books, 2008.

Vanderkam, Laura. "Here's Why Unlimited Vacation May Be Too Good to Be True." *Fortune.* October 3, 2015.

Washburn, David, and Adam Elmahrek. "Banked Vacation and Sick Leave Lead to Big Payouts." Voice of OC. September 30, 2013. http://voiceofoc.org/2013/09/banked-vacation-and-sick-leave-lead-to-big-payouts/.

Weisberg, Anne. "The Workplace Culture That Flying Nannies Won't Fix." *New York Times.* Opinion Page. August 24, 2015.

CHAPTER 6: BANK EQUITY WITH YOUR LABOR FORCE

"APA Survey Finds Feeling Valued at Work Linked to Well-Being and Performance." American Psychological Association. March 8, 2012. http://www.apa.org/news/press/releases/2012/03/well-being.aspx.

"Dale Carnegie Training Uncovers Major Drivers of Employee Engagement in US Workforce." Business Wire. February 11, 2013. http://www.businesswire.com/news/home/20130211005999/en/Dale-Carnegie-Training-Uncovers-Major-Drivers-Employee.

D'Onfro, Jillian. "Here Are All of Google's Employee Perks, and How Much They Cost the Company." *Business Insider.* April 7, 2015.

Mika, Shelley. "The Four Drivers of Innovation." Gallup Business Journal. January 11, 2007. http://www.gallup.com/businessjournal/26068/four-drivers-innovation.aspx.

Sherman Garr, Stacia. *The Employee Recognition Maturity Model: A Roadmap to Strategic Recognition*. Oakland, CA: Bersin & Associates, November 2, 2012.

Sinek, Simon. *Leaders Eat Last: Why Some Teams Pull Together and Others Don't*. New York: Portfolio, 2014.

Sweeney, Deborah. "3 Ways Handwritten Notes Impact the Workplace." *Forbes*, April 24, 2012.

Chapter 7: Optimize and Exploit Diversity

2015 Hollywood Diversity Report: Flipping the Script. Los Angeles: Ralph J. Bunche Center for African American Studies at UCLA, 2015. http://www.bunchecenter.ucla.edu/wp-content/uploads/2015/02/2015-Hollywood-Diversity-Report-2-25-15.pdf.

Block, Laszlo. "Getting to Work on Diversity at Google." Google Official Blog. May 28, 2014. https://googleblog.blogspot.com/2014/05/getting-to-work-on-diversity-at-google.html.

Brooks, Alison Wood, Laura Huang, Fiona Murray, and Sarah Wood Kearney. "Investors Prefer Entrepreneurial Ventures Pitched by Attractive Men." *Proceedings of the National Academy of Sciences* 111, no. 12 (March 25, 2014): 4427–31.

"DGA TV Diversity Report: Employer Hiring of Women Directors Shows Modest Improvement; Women and Minorities Continue to Be Excluded in First-Time Hiring." Directors Guild of America. August 25, 2015. http://www.dga.org/news/pressreleases/2015/150825-episodic-director-diversity-report.aspx.

Janis, Irving L. *Victims of Groupthink: A Psychological Study of Foreign-Policy Decisions and Fiascoes*. Boston: Houghton Mifflin, 1972.

Phillips, Katherine W. "How Diversity Makes Us Smarter." *Scientific American*. September 16, 2014.

Rivera, Lauren A. "Hiring as Cultural Matching: The Case of Elite Professional Service Firms." *American Sociological Review* 77, no. 6 (December 2012): 999–1022.

Romero, Dennis. "How Hollywood Keeps Minorities Out." *LA Weekly*. February 25, 2015.

US Census Bureau. http://www.census.gov.

Weise, Elizabeth, and Jessica Guynn. "Tech Jobs: Minorities Have Degrees, but Don't Get Hired." *USA Today*. October 13, 2014.

Wolfe, Lahle. "Trends and Statistics for Women in Business: Using Industry Trends and Business Growth Statistics to Grow Your Own Business." About Money. http://womeninbusiness.about.com/od /wibtrendsandstatistics/a/wibtrendsnstats.htm.

CHAPTER 8: FIND THE HARD CORNERS

Charity Navigator. http://www.charitynavigator.org.

Finkelstein, Sydney, Jo Whitehead, and Andrew Campbell. "Think Again: Why Good Leaders Make Bad Decisions and How to Keep It from Happening to You." *Harvard Business Review Press*. January 6, 2009.

Green, C. Shawn, Alexandre Pouget, and Daphne Bavelier. "Improved Probabilistic Inference as a General Learning Mechanism with Action Video Games." *Current Biology* 20, no. 17 (September 14, 2010): 1573–9.

Hammonds, Keith H. "The Strategy of the Fighter Pilot." FastCompany. May 31, 2002. http://www.fastcompany.com/44983/strategy-fighter -pilot.

Hippocrates. "The History of Epidemics." *Hippocratic Corpus*. 1780.

Iyengar, Sheena, and Kanika Agrawal. "A Better Choosing Experience: When Consumers Are Overwhelmed with Options, Marketers Should Give Them What They Really Want: Ways of Shopping That Lower the Cognitive Stress." *Strategy+Business*. Winter 2010.

Kotler, Steven. "Cognitive Warming: Brain Training for High Pressure Decision-Making." *Forbes*. September 17, 2014.

Lehrer, Johna. " 'Deliberate Calm' Guided US Airways Crew." *Los Angeles Times*. January 17, 2009.

McGrath, Rita Gunther. "Transient Advantage." *Harvard Business Review*. June 2013.

Morewedge, Carey K. "How a Video Game Helped People Make Better Decisions." *Harvard Business Review*. October 13, 2015.

Pfau, Michael W., and James P. Dillard. *The Persuasion Handbook: Developments in Theory and Practice*. Thousand Oaks, CA: SAGE Publications, 2002.

"The Tyranny of Choice. You Choose. If You Can Have Everything in 57 Varieties, Making Decisions Becomes Hard Work." *Economist*. December 16, 2010.

White, Erin. "Why Good Managers Make Bad Decisions." *Wall Street Journal*. February 14, 2009.

CHAPTER 9: ADOPT A CRISIS-MANAGEMENT MODEL

60 Minutes. CBS. November 22, 2015.

The Global Benefits Attitudes Survey 2013. Arlington, VA: Towers Watson, 2013.

The Global Benefits Attitudes Survey 2014. Arlington, VA: Towers Watson, 2014.

Grossman, Dave, and Loren W. Christensen. *On Combat*. Warrior Science Publications, 2008.

Higginbottom, Karen. "Workplace Stress Leads to Less Productive Employees." *Forbes*. September 11, 2014.

CHAPTER 10: REMEMBER TO LEAD AS WELL AS MANAGE

Anthony, Scott, David S. Duncan, and Pontus M. A. Siren. "Zombie Projects: How to Find Them and Kill Them." *Harvard Business Review*. March 4, 2015.

Friedman, Roger. "Altman: *Titanic* Worst Movie Ever." Fox News Channel. March 23, 2002.

Godwin, Christopher. "James Cameron: From *Titanic* to *Avatar*." *Times* (London). November 8, 2008.

Olshan, Jeremy, and Ikimulisa Livingston. "Quiet Air Hero Is Captain America." *New York Post*. January 17, 2009.

"The Shocking Truth: The U.S. Medical System Is Woefully Unprepared for Ebola." Washington's Blog, October 3, 2014. http://www.washingtonsblog.com/2014/10/shocking-truth-u-s-medical-system-prepared-ebola.html.

INDEX

———★———